Who the Hell is Michel Foucault?

Who the Hell is Michel Foucault?

And what are his theories all about?

Dr Julian Molina

**BOWDEN
&BRAZIL**

First published in Great Britain in 2021 by
Bowden & Brazil Ltd
Felixstowe, Suffolk, UK.

British Library Cataloguing-in-Publication Data
A CIP record for this book is available from The British Library.

Series editor & academic advisor: Dr. Jonathan C.P. Birch, University of Glasgow.

ISBN 978-1-8382286-1-3

To find out more about other books and authors in this series,
visit www.whothehellis.co.uk

Contents

Introduction

Shortly before his death, Michel Foucault re-read the journals of Franz Kafka. For several months he had been aware that his health had been worsening and that he was close to death. He asked doctors how long he had left and remarked that it was 'too late' to do any further work on his historical studies. Perhaps he had read some of the last entries in Kafka's diaries, in which he reflected upon his 'horrible spells', the hypocrisy of writing about his illness and being 'incapable of anything but pain'.

Foucault published his first book, *Mental Illness and Personality* (1954), around 30 years earlier. Starting from this publication, he began to examine the history of scientific knowledge and the human sciences. These sciences are fundamentally different from the scientific study of planets, plants or weather systems, and they originate from the European Age of Enlightenment. This was an intellectual movement in the 17th and 18th centuries whose proponents championed the use of reason, observation and the scientific method, intending these principles to produce knowledge that would supersede superstition and dogma.

Throughout his life, Foucault examined the human sciences – psychology, sociology, linguistics, economics and biology.

Although we may believe that these sciences discovered truth about humans and dispelled myths from a pre-scientific age, Foucault cautioned us to be wary of the idea that these sciences have produced objective knowledge about a universal subject. Rather, he warned, this belief acts to mask other truths which have become hidden and excluded.

In *Mental Illness and Personality*, Foucault demonstrated what it means to explore the relationship between scientific knowledge and the conditions of human existence. This book follows these paths and asks some simple questions. How were the human sciences born? What are the instruments of analysis used by these sciences? What are these sciences' fictions, techniques and artifices? How do these sciences relate to power, law, punishment and control?

In Foucault's first books on mental illness and madness, he wrote about how the science of psychology developed cultural frameworks for understanding and treating madness. His books offer a crucial insight into how our cultural and scientific understanding of mental illness is not historically stable. Knowledge of madness changes over time, as new criteria replace old; new forms of mental illnesses are 'discovered', classified and named; and new ideas about madness become part of our cultural landscape.

Foucault argued that psychology did not reveal the truth of madness but excluded lives which were considered abnormal. An important theme throughout Foucault's philosophical works is how Western Enlightenment thought has concealed and excluded other histories. What Foucault did was to find and write these hidden histories. These are the histories of human sciences, confinement, and the technologies of power that emerged from the 16th century in the form of asylums, prisons and colonial imperialism.

Foucault's historical studies covered a wide terrain. He published works on prisons and factories, the role of psychology in legal proceedings, the history of sexuality, and practices for interpreting the self. He also wrote about real historical figures who were excluded from triumphant accounts of scientific achievements and liberal democracies. These were persons who were considered abnormal in terms of their sexuality; they were 'moral monsters', 'disorderly families', and individuals that required punishment.

As for Foucault's reputation during his lifetime, it would be no exaggeration to say that he was already a cultural icon by the mid-1960s. Perhaps the most well-known public intellectual to have emerged from the so-called generation of *Soixante-Huitard* philosophers who supported French protesters in the summer of 1968. His annual lectures at the Collège de France, where he taught from 1971 to 1984, were attended by thousands.

The influence of Foucault's philosophy has only grown with his passing. His works have been widely translated and nearly all of his lecture courses at the Collège de France have been transcribed and published with accompanying course summaries. The academic journal *Foucault Studies* published its 27th issue in December 2019. He has been the subject of several biographies and documentary films, and his work is required reading for students of philosophy, history, literature, criminology and many other subjects in the humanities and social sciences.

This book begins by looking at Foucault's life and the influences upon his thinking, providing some context with which to understand his ideas about knowledge, power and the human subject. Here we learn about Foucault's involvement in various political groups and his collaboration with other historians and philosophers. The book then goes on to examine three of Foucault's key ideas, offering a starting point for the reader to further examine other hidden histories that Foucault so furiously revealed.

1. Foucault's Life Story

There is some irony in writing about Foucault's life in order to understand the context from which his ideas arose, because he made his feelings known on this point, stating that his life story was irrelevant to discussions about his work. He was resistant to the notion that an author's ideas sprang from either their psychological disposition or life experiences. Prior to an interview with a Dutch television broadcaster, he wrote a letter stipulating that biographical information should not be included in the documentary.

> *'Sir, I do not wish that during the television broadcast you want to devote to me, any biographical information be given any place. I consider indeed such information to have no importance for the subject matter at hand. Yours sincerely, Michel Foucault.'* (Foucault, 2012)

During a debate with the American linguist and philosopher Noam Chomsky (1928–), Foucault declined to directly answer a question about his own personal creativity, saying that the problem of personal experience is not very important. He argued that scientific discoveries and knowledge should not be attributed to a single, identifiable individual, but are due to complex, multiple forces. Although biographers have narrated the events in Foucault's life, bringing together his personal life with his philosophical works, Foucault himself said that he did not philosophize in order to represent the world. 'One writes to become someone other than who one is'. So, who was Michel Foucault and who did he become?

A Childhood Disrupted by War

Paul-Michel Foucault was born at 10 rue de la Visitation, Poitiers, France, on 15 October 1926. He was the middle child of three children, having an older sister, Francine, who was born 18 months before him, and a younger brother, Denys, born five years later. The Foucault family tradition was to name their eldest son Paul. Paul-Michel's father, Paul-André Foucault, was born in 1893, and he was the son and grandson of medical doctors. Paul-André taught at a medical school in Poitiers and was a surgeon of high standing, sometimes operating on people in their homes (he was known for travelling with a folding operating table). Foucault's mother, Anne-Marie Foucault, was also the daughter of a surgeon, and wanted to train as a medic herself, but at the time the profession was barred to women. Anne-Marie was independently wealthy, owned land, and ran a household of several servants as well as her husband's medical practice.

Foucault's lifelong partner, Daniel Defert (1937–), said that Foucault seldom talked about his father, who was tormented by anxiety. Like a good many surgeons at the time, he could only operate by resorting to powerful stimulants. Foucault may not have wanted to speak about his father but he made many allusions to him when talking about his relation to writing, referring to the scalpel and the pen, for instance. 'I imagine my pen-nib has some inherited vestige of the scalpel' he said to interviewer Claude Bonnefoy in 2011 (Bonnefoy, 2011).

Fig. 1 Daniel Defert

The family were members of the rural bourgeoisie, and from 1936–45 employed an English nanny 'to speak with the children' (Delfert, in Falzon et al, 2013). They owned both a large house in Poitiers and a villa by the sea, in La Baule, Brittany, where they spent the summer every year. Paul-Michel and his siblings would while away the hours on the beach, playing tennis and going cycling. This continued until war broke out in late 1939, when France and the UK declared war on Germany. In May 1940, the Germans broke through the Maginot line – a line of fortifications along 750 km of the French border – and medical units were set up in Poitiers to care for the wounded soldiers. Foucault's father's skills as a doctor were heavily called upon, as were his mother's considerable organizational skills. On 17 June 1940, France negotiated an armistice with Germany, and Poitiers became part of the occupied zone, with German soldiers patrolling the streets. The villa in La Baule was requisitioned for officers of the occupying forces, and at school the children (including Paul-Michel) were taught to sing '*Travail, famille, patrie*', which translates as 'Work, family, homeland' and was the tripartite motto introduced by the Vichy regime. The

French were told they should regard all earlier forms of French culture as 'egotistical, individualist, bourgeois' and children were encouraged to embrace a new world 'of solidarity and sacrifice' (Macey, 1993). Foucault later recalled the arrests of citizens by armed soldiers on the street, and the silent crowds who watched as the people were taken away.

None of the family were supportive of the Vichy regime, but they were forced to comply with its requirements. Food became scarce, and Foucault's mother Anne-Marie was often forced to cycle into the countryside to buy food on the black market. Rationing had made transportation by car impossible.

A Serious Education

Children in France usually started school at the age of six, but Paul-Michel refused to be separated from his sister Francine when she first went to school, so he attended from the age of four. Although he was often left to his own devices, he learned to read and write from an early age, and soon understood that his sense of identity would be tied to his academic ambitions. As he said in later life, schooling and competition went hand in hand: 'The rule of promotion lay in knowledge, in knowing a bit more than the others, being a bit better in the classroom' (Miller, 2000). The school, Lycée Henri-IV in Poitiers, was run by Jesuits, and the seriousness with which the Foucault children's education was provided was matched in attitude at home. Paul-Michel and his sister were taught to believe that although wealth could be inherited, a successful career depended upon qualifications and skills. This was to be their first introduction to an elite world, attending a fee-paying school that represented the first rung on a ladder which would inevitably lead to university and professional qualifications.

Foucault was not known to make a great effort in school, but his quick mind served him well, particularly in studying French, Latin, Greek and history. However, after four years at Henri-IV, he failed his end-of-year exams and was told he would need to retake them the following term. His mother chose instead to transfer him to a different school: the Collège Saint-Stanislas in Poitiers. Here his work and grades improved, but his sense of self and his environment had been profoundly altered due to the war, and he struggled to find equilibrium. Recalling his childhood during an interview in 1982, he said,

> *'what strikes me now when I try to recall those impressions is that nearly all the great emotional memories I have are related to the political situation [...] I remember very well that I experienced one of my first great frights when Chancellor Dollfuss was assassinated by the Nazis [...] it was my first strong fright about death. I also remember refugees from Spain arriving in Poitiers [...] I remember fighting [...] with classmates about the Ethiopian War. I think that boys and girls of this generation had their childhood formed by these great historical events. The menace of war was our background, our framework of existence. Then the war arrived.'* (Foucault, 1994)

He became interested in philosophy, but on the first day of formal philosophy lessons, his schoolteacher was arrested by the Gestapo for his work in the French Resistance network and

Fig. 2 École Normale Supérieure, Paris.

was never seen again. Foucault said that during this period in France, 'private life was really threatened' (1994). Looking back, he said that 'I don't think I ever had the project of becoming a philosopher […] We did not know when I was ten or eleven years old whether we would become German or remain French. We did not know whether we would die or not in the bombing and so on.' (Foucault, 1994)

Once Foucault finished his secondary education, his lack of ambition to go to university conflicted with his father's hopes that he would take over the family practice. This led to noisy, sometimes violent arguments between father and son, and a long-lasting cooling of their relationship. Foucault had never shown any great interest in natural sciences and he refused any suggestion that he would study medicine. His father eventually settled on persuading Paul-Michel's brother Denys to become the next doctor in the family and allowed Paul-Michel to indulge his vague ambitions of a career in either politics or journalism. Though Foucault would stay close to his mother all his life, he never regained a good relationship with his father.

University and the Onset of Depression

By 1943, he had set his sights on studying at the École Normale Supérieure (ENS) in Paris, one of the so-called 'Grand Schools' of France and the most prestigious university in the country at the time. But first he had to return to his old lycée, Henri-IV in Poitiers, to prepare for the entrance examinations. Here he studied philosophy, reading the works of Henri Bergson (1859–1941) and René Descartes (1596–1650), and was known as a hard-working student, his days largely dominated by reading. He voraciously read literature during this time, particularly the works of Honoré de Balzac (1799–1850) and Stendhal (1783–1842), as well as André Gide (1869–1951), including his book, *Le Séquestrée de Poitiers* (translated as 'The Confined Woman of Poitiers') (1930).

Foucault later spoke of walking past a courtyard in Poitiers where a young woman had been imprisoned in a locked room by her family for 25 years, after having conceived an illegitimate child. This true, infamous case was the focus of Gide's book, which documented the case from many angles, capturing the perspectives and words of all those involved, from the woman herself to her captors, the police and the court. Gide's book was said to have influenced Foucault greatly, and it bears many similarities to a book of his own that focused on the many discourses (words, perspectives) around an infamous murder that took place in 1836: *I, Pierre Rivière* (1975).

In 1945, after failing the entrance exam for the École Normale, Foucault enrolled in the Lycée Henri-IV in the Latin Quarter of Paris to prepare to retake the examination. This prestigious school had also been attended by the renowned philosophers Jean-Paul Sartre (1905–80), Simone Weil (1909–43), and Gilles Deleuze (1925–95), and the authors André Gide, Pierre Loti (1850–1923), Guy de Maupassant (1850–93), among other illustrious names. Foucault did not board at Henri-IV, but lived with a family friend, which allowed him to escape from the rituals of communal living but was not luxurious accommodation. It was unheated and Foucault had to wrap himself in blankets in order to keep warm enough to work.

In 1946 Foucault passed the entrance exam and finally gained admission to the École Normale in Paris. It was here that he met the Marxist philosopher Louis Althusser (1918–90), who was affectionately referred to as 'old Alt', and who became a tutor at the university while Foucault was there. Althusser was only eight years older than Foucault but, having gained entrance to the École Normale in 1939, he had been drafted into the army and spent five years in a prisoner-of-war camp in Germany, before returning to the École in 1945, aged 27. His communist viewpoint (formed during the war) was very influential on Foucault. The philosopher and psychologist Maurice Merleau-Ponty (1908–61) also became a tutor at the École during Foucault's time there, and his course on the union of mind and body, as argued by Malebranche and Bergson, would also be instrumental in Foucault's early intellectual thinking.

Foucault had difficulty adjusting to the communal living at the university and to an educational system that segregated the arts from the sciences. It was also a highly competitive environment and he experienced severe bouts of depression during this period. He drank heavily and was rumoured to be taking drugs, and there were even reports of an attempted suicide. It has been widely suggested that his deep depression was due to coming to terms with his homosexuality, but the trauma he suffered as a child in wartime France is likely to have also played a part. The two factors collided in 1942, when Marshal Henri-Philippe Pétain (head of state under the German occupation) amended Article 334 of the penal code so that anyone who, 'to satisfy his own passions, commits one or several shameless or unnatural acts with a minor of his own sex under the age of 21' would be fined and serve a prison term of six months to three years. Foucault was 16 years old at the time.

After the liberation of France, the provisional government under Charles de Gaulle affirmed this anti-homosexual legislation by issuing an ordinance in 1945, saying: 'The principal motive of this [1942] reform, inspired by a concern to prevent the corruption of minors, cannot be criticized.' Althusser counselled Foucault against hospitalization for his depression, and offered him friendly support, but at the same time would occasionally make Foucault the target of his biting humour. Upon hearing that Foucault had been spending time at a psychiatric hospital in order to study madness for his dissertation, Althusser remarked that Foucault should be kept there.

Throughout all this, Foucault was nonetheless known as a diligent student who neatly stored his copious notes in boxes. In 1948 he gained a BA degree in philosophy, and in 1949 took a further degree in psychology. Anxiety and depression were constant problems at this time, which Foucault attempted to alleviate with alcohol. He began studying for the agrégation (qualifying exam for university teachers) in philosophy. He failed at his first attempt to sit the exam in 1950 and this worried his fellow students, who suggested that Foucault was the victim of a communist witch hunt (though Foucault's record in passing exams had always been variable). In October 1950 he underwent a brief detoxification treatment, and in August 1951 he finally passed the *agrégation*, after having been examined on the topic of sexuality.

Prisons and Asylums

After passing his *agrégation*, Foucault went on to complete a diploma course in psychopathology taught at the Institut de Psychologie in Paris. He practised as a psychologist in Professor Jean Delay's unit there, attending hospitals and lectures (on psychological theory and psychoanalysis). He later said that his research on madness derived from his curiosity about studying 'what madness was'. He was associated with the National d'Orientation at Fresnes, a prison that housed the medical facilities for the French penitentiary system. This facility gathered information in order to assess prisoners' risk. Foucault was based in a unit that assessed whether prisoners had 'real or simulated' psychopathological disorders.

Foucault was a regular attendee at Sainte-Anne, a psychiatric hospital in Paris, where he witnessed public examinations of patients. About his time at Sainte-Anne, Foucault said:

> *'There was no clear professional status for psychologists*
> *in a mental hospital. So as a student in psychology [...]*
> *I had a very strange status there. The 'chef de service'*

Fig. 3 Sainte-Anne Psychiatric Hospital, Paris.

[Jean Delay] was very kind to me and let me do anything I wanted. But nobody worried about what I should be doing; I was free to do anything. I was actually in a position between the staff and the patients.'
(Foucault, 1994)

At this time Foucault began an intense relationship with the composer Jean Barraqué (1928–73). An important figure in contemporary music, Foucault described him in a letter to a friend as 'adorable, ugly as sin, terribly spiritual, his knowledge of bad boys touched on the encyclopedic. I was completely disconcerted at feeling called by him to explore a world of which I yet knew nothing, and where my suffering would surely follow me.' (Cited in the 'Chrononogy' of Foucault's *Dits et Ecrits*, 1994.)

In June of 1952 Foucault completed his diploma in Psychopathology at the Institut. In October, at the invitation of Raymond Pollin, a friend of Althusser, he moved to the psychology department in Lille. Here he was commended for his excellent teaching; the dean of the faculty wrote that he was: 'very dynamic. Organizes the teaching of scientific psychology with talent. Truly merits promotion.' (Miller, 2000) Around this time, Foucault began working on his first book, *Mental Illness and Personality*, which was commissioned by Althusser as part of a series of books aimed at students. Published in 1954, it contains sketches of many of the ideas that would appear in his later cultural and social histories of madness.

Foucault was not altogether forthcoming about this research. One of his friends in Lille, the surrealist Maurice Pinguet (1929–91), noted that Foucault would rarely elaborate upon his research or the preparation of his manuscript. This was a pattern that others would come to expect when talking with Foucault about his research, either at the Bibliothèque Nationale or elsewhere. The best that Pinguet said he could expect was either a smile or an anecdote, without any in-depth discussion of the subject matter that so consumed the young philosopher.

In 1953, Pinguet and Foucault drove together to Rome. Pinguet noted that 'Hegel, Marx, Heidegger, Freud' were Foucault's 'axes of reference' when his 'encounter with Nietzsche occurred [...] I can see Michel reading [Nietzsche's] *Untimely Meditations* in the sun, on the beach...' (Defert, 2013). On the back of the typescript of *Mental Illness and Personality*, Foucault wrote 'There are three related experiences: the dream, drunkenness, and madness', referring to Nietzsche's exploration of the wilder parts of ourselves. Later, he added, 'All the Apollonian qualities defined in [Nietzsche's] *The Birth of Tragedy* form the free and luminous space of philosophical existence' (Falzon et al, 2013).

Foucault left France for Uppsala, Sweden, in 1955, taking up a position as a cultural diplomat and university instructor. He said the reason for his departure was due to his suffering:

'I have suffered and I will suffer from a lot of things in French social and cultural life [...] Well, I think that, at the moment when I left France, freedom for personal life was very sharply restricted there. At this time Sweden was supposed to be a much freer country.' (Miller, 2000)

Despite Foucault's hopes to live a freer life, he found that Sweden's 'freedoms' were actually repressive. 'A certain kind of freedom,' he said, could have 'as many restrictive effects as a directly repressive society' (Foucault, 1963). He remarked that Sweden was an 'overly medicalized' society, and the University of Uppsala proved to be both rigidly hierarchical and puritanical in outlook. He began drinking heavily again during this time, and impulsively bought a beige Jaguar sports car – an expensive purchase for a junior faculty member. While in Sweden, he was also appointed director of the Maison de France, a cultural relations outpost of a Parisian government department. Here he was responsible for arranging cultural events, such as performances, poetry readings and plays, and he invited guest speakers such as the novelists and critics Marguerite Duras (1914–96), Roland Barthes (1915–80), Claude Simon (1913–2005) and Jean Hyppolite (1907–68).

In October 1958, Foucault moved to Poland, a now-communist country that was still largely in ruins following World War II. Here he took up a post at Warsaw University, undertaking responsibility for reopening their French Cultural Centre. He stayed in the Bristol Hotel, above a café that acted as a meeting place for the intellectuals of Warsaw. It was the most upmarket hotel in Warsaw and also the most infiltrated by the secret service, who commonly bugged the rooms (Sobolczyk, 2018). During the evenings Foucault worked by candlelight on a manuscript. His days were full – in Poland he had agreed to undertake similar responsibilities to those he had held in Sweden, acting as a cultural diplomat, while also teaching topics related to contemporary theatre as well as French-language classes. He was involved in activities at the French embassy and took the opportunity to travel and lecture throughout Poland, speaking about intellectuals such as the French poet Guillaume Apollinaire. However, the country was run by an authoritarian regime that was hostile to free-thinking and homosexuality, and when the authorities became aware of Foucault's research and manuscripts on imprisonment, they sought a way to discredit and deport him. They arranged for a young male agent named Jurek to meet with him, with the aim of seducing him. According to Sobolczyk, 'Jurek was straight and then married with children' but had probably been forced into becoming an agent because of his father's anticommunist activities. During the encounter with Jurek, the Polish secret service entered the room and told Foucault to leave the country or face imprisonment. They also threatened the French embassy with the 'scandal' and forced them to expel Foucault from Poland.

Foucault returned to France in October 1959, shortly after the death of his father. He carried with him the products of several years of research, including a translation of Kant's *Anthropology from a Pragmatic Point of View* (1798) and a manuscript of 943 pages. This manuscript would allow him to attain his doctorate under the title *Folie et Déraison: Histoire de la folie à l'âge classique* (translated as 'Madness and Civilization: A history of insanity in the age of reason') and would become his first major book, published that same year. He passed the public defence of his thesis, the soutenance de thèse, on 20 May 1961. Two months later, using the inheritance his father had left him, he purchased his first apartment on the rue du Docteur Finlay, Paris. His long-term partner, Daniel Defert, described the apartment, which was perched at the top of a brand-new building, as seeming to have been furnished by either a scientist or a protestant pastor from Sweden.

Finding the Right Language

During the early 1960s, Foucault began to establish his reputation in France after the publication of *Madness and Civilization* (1961). In May 1962 he was appointed professor of psychology at the University of Clermont-Ferrand, and in the same month took part in a conference on 'Heresy and Society in Pre-Industrial Europe'. He began to lecture widely about medical knowledge and was invited to lecture at universities in Denmark and Belgium. As well as lecturing, he wrote magazine articles and book reviews, largely focusing on literature, such as an article on Jean-Pierre Brisset in the *Nouvelle Revue Française*. In January 1963, he joined Roland Barthes and Michel Deguy (1930–) on the editorial board of the literary and philosophical journal, *Critique*. He also published *Naissance de la Clinique: Une archéologie du regard médical* (translated as 'The Birth of the Clinic: An Archaeology of Medical Perception') in April 1963. The following month he published his only work on literature,

Death and the Labyrinth: The World of Raymond Roussel (1963). Roussel was a French poet, novelist and playwright, and an influential figure on surrealist fiction.

Foucault's growing reputation began to lead to critical scrutiny of his work. One of his former students from ENS, Jacques Derrida, gave a lecture in March 1963 on 'The Cogito and the History of Madness'. With Foucault in attendance, Derrida critiqued Foucault's reading of René Descartes in his *Madness and Civilization*. Derrida challenged Foucault's claims to have written a history of madness, arguing that he had misinterpreted Descartes' ideas on madness, ignoring key materials in *Meditations on First Philosophy* (1641). Instead, Derrida claimed, Foucault stayed within the limits of reason. Foucault did not respond to these criticisms until 1970 and in the meantime held a truce with Derrida while they both sat on the editorial board of *Critique*. After Foucault's death, Derrida spoke of their friendship and their decade-long argument in *The Work of Mourning* (2001):

> '*Thirty years ago the publication of this great book of Foucault's [Madness and Civilization] was an event whose repercussions were so intense and multiple that I will not even try to identify them, much less measure them, deep inside me. Next, because I love friendship, and the trusting affection that Foucault showed me thirty years ago, which was to last for many years, was all the more precious in that, being shared, it corresponded to my professed admiration for him.*' (Derrida 2003)

Foucault continued to travel during the 1960s. While visiting Madrid, Spain, he visited the Museo Nacional del Prado, which held the works of the 17th-century Spanish painter, Diego Velázquez, including *Las Meninas* (1656). In an interview with critic Claude Bonnefoy in 1968, Foucault described how he studied this painting for several hours, and then 'one day [...] I had this urge to write about the painting from memory, to describe what was in it'. He realized that he had found

> 'exactly the right language by which the distance between ourselves and the classical philosophy of representation and classical ideas of order and resemblance could come into focus and be evaluated. That's how I began to write *The Order of Things.*' (Foucault, Artieres et al., 2016b)

Foucault would finish writing *The Order of Things* in May 1965, writing to his partner, Daniel Defert, 'Finally finished the thing. Three hundred pages re-written, in a completely different balance, since Sfax [city in Tunisia]' (Defert, 2013). This book would feature in Jean-Luc Godard's film, *La Chinoise* (1967), which shows a student throwing tomatoes at a copy of the book as it was thought to symbolize the opposite of revolution. It was also a bestseller – the first print run sold out in six weeks. Foucault was now a household name, and phrases from the book such as 'the death of man' and 'Marxism exists in 19th-century thought like a fish in water' (because 'it is unable to breathe anywhere else') became common currency.

Participating in Student Revolts

The following autumn (1966), Foucault moved to Tunisia, where he had been offered a teaching position at the University of Tunis. He went camping with donkeys and camels in southern

Algeria for Christmas, travelling on the Tassili-n-Ajjer plateau. Besides teaching in Tunis, Foucault prepared the manuscript for *The Archaeology of Knowledge*. Although published in 1969, much of this text concerned Foucault's earlier works on madness, clinical medicine and the human sciences, and his methodological approach towards language and existence. In Tunisia, Foucault was also a regular speaker at a cultural centre, Club Tahar Hadad.

While teaching at the university, Foucault became close to his students, supporting many of whom were involved in socialist protests. Some were arrested and tortured by the Tunisian state; those that remained free began secretly printing their pamphlets in Foucault's apartment. Rather than the popular protests and events across France in May 1968, it was Foucault's involvement in the Tunisian student movement in March 1968 which encouraged a more politically engaged philosophy.

> '*I remember that [Herbert] Marcuse said reproachfully one day, where was Foucault at the time of the May barricades? Well, I was in Tunisia, on account of my work. And I must add that this experience was a decisive one for me [...] Tunisia, for me, represented in some ways the chance to reinsert myself in the political debate. It wasn't May of '68 in France that changed me; it was March of '68, in a third-world country.*' (Foucault quoted in Medien, 2019)

In the spring of 1968, Foucault read Rosa Luxemburg and Che Guevara, while student demonstrations erupted in Warsaw, Madrid and Rome. He met with President Bourguiba of Tunisia and the French Ambassador to Tunisia to defend the students and other activists. Back in France, he was criticized for not leaving Tunisia during the protests and the subsequent arrests of French students.

In April 1970, Foucault was nominally elected as the chair in what he called the History of Systems of Thought at the Collège de France. That December, he gave his inaugural lecture on 'The Order of Discourse'. This began Foucault's series of lectures at the Collège, which he continued to deliver for the next 14 years. In these lectures he presented sketches of the historical studies that he was working on and examined issues related to both power and knowledge, as they manifested in his studies of sovereignty, psychiatric power, security, and the defence of society. His first course focused on the work of the German philosopher Friedrich Nietzsche and his idea of the 'Will to Knowledge'.

Revolutionary 70s

During the 1970s, Foucault took part in demonstrations and political activities on numerous issues. He demonstrated against the war in Vietnam, the police, prisons, the criminal justice system, and the racism and hostility towards immigrants in France. His militant activism took the form of writing open letters, signing political petitions, supporting people in criminal trials and press conferences, and appearing in court to give evidence. In 1971, for instance, he was contacted by lawyers acting for Christian Riss, a militant activist who had been shot at point-blank range by police during demonstrations outside the Jordanian embassy in Paris. Along with philosopher-writers Jean-Marie Domenach (1922–97) and Maurice Clavel

(1920–79), Foucault gave a press conference that acted as a *comité de défense* (defence committee) for Riss.

Between 1971 and 1973, Foucault's attention was acutely focused on political activities with the *Group d'Information sur les Prisons* (the Group for Information on the Prisons), commonly referred to as the GIP. In February 1971, he announced its creation, coinciding this announcement with a press conference in support of Maoist activists who were on hunger strike in France, and called for them to be recognized as political prisoners rather than criminals. He agreed to take an instrumental role in the GIP's activities to attack the prison system.

The GIP began a series of 'intolerability inquiries' focused on what was 'intolerable' about the current state of prisons. The group collected and publicized information, testimony and evidence from prisoners about prison conditions (see Chapter 4). Their first pamphlet, an 'Inquiry into Twenty Prisons', was published without any indication that Foucault was involved in the arrangement of the text. That November, Foucault rented a large theatre to screen a film for several thousand people about two US prisons, Soledad and San Quentin, and invited the families of convicted criminals and former inmates.

This was a period of intense political activity across France, with prison riots, factory takeovers by workers, the killings of Maoist militants, political kidnappings, and the establishment of several other groups focused on health, asylum, and migrant workers. During the 1970s he also began to develop a new understanding of power and knowledge, and his accounts particularly focused on how they operated in relation to both prisons and the state. Most concretely he began to prepare, what he called, a 'book on punishment'. His work with the GIP was important for developing many of the ideas that he would present in his book, *Surveiller et Punir: Naissance de la prison* (translated as 'Discipline and Punish: The Birth of the Prison'), published in 1975. While preparing this manuscript, he also taught courses on prisons and punishment at the Collège de France, including a lecture series on 'Penal Theories and Institutions' in November 1971 and 'The Punitive Society' in January 1973.

In April 1975, Foucault made his first visit to California, after being invited to the Department of French Literature at the University of California, Berkeley. He would continue to visit California and teach at Berkeley until the 1980s. His longtime partner, Daniel Defert, said it was during this trip to California that Foucault discovered 'the hedonistic culture developed by Californians around drugs' (Defert, 2013). Foucault took LSD at Zabriske Point in Death Valley, writing in a letter: 'drugs – a break with this physics of power, work, consumption, localization'. Didier Eribon, a fellow French philosopher and friend of Foucault's, wrote: 'Foucault's American happiness: a reconciliation with himself is finally realized. He is happy in his work. He is happy in the pleasures of his body.' (Eribon, 1992) Eribon went on to say that, from the beginning of the 1980s, Foucault seriously considered leaving France and moving to the USA.

Throughout the last decade of Foucault's life, he concentrated on preparing his *History of Sexuality* (1976–2018). He is reported to have begun writing the first of these volumes on the same day that he completed *Discipline and Punish*. In a letter, Foucault wrote that 'My outcasts are incredibly familiar and repetitive. I want to work on other things: political economy, strategy, politics' (Defert, 2013). The six-volume *History of Sexuality* was announced in November 1976, in the French newspaper, *Le Monde*. Accompanying the announcement, a short piece appeared on the front page of the newspaper:

> '*Sex repressed? We go on saying it again and again: the West has supposedly smothered, censured and forbidden the healthy exercise of healthy pleasure. And sexual liberation, which has become necessary, would apparently be both felicitous and subversive. Michel Foucault, professor at the Collège de France and one of the 'great gurus' of our young philosophers, now rejects that hypothesis as a received idea.*' (Macey, 2019)

The publishers intended to publish one volume each year, while (according to some reports) Foucault planned a volume to be published every three months. He began to prepare the research folders for each volume.

On his desk there was a voluminous folder for each of the titles planned, awaiting the hour of its definitive elaboration, the moment when Foucault's prose – beautiful and precise, meticulously worked – would take hold of the material inside to transfigure it. A manuscript written by Foucault is immediately distinguishable as belonging to him from the almost-undecipherable handwriting, which is loaded with additions and scratched out words (Eribon, 1992).

By the time of Foucault's death in 1984, only three of the six volumes had been published. A fourth was posthumously published in 2018, under the title of *Confessions of the Flesh*. The main themes of these works were the relationship between sex, truth and power, with a focus on Greek, Romans, and early Christian thinkers. Over the late 1970s and 1980s, there were various proposals and plans for the different volumes. Initially, the planned series of books would encompass volumes on *The Will to Knowledge, The Flesh and the Body, The Children's Crusade, The Woman, the Mother, and the Hysteric, The Perverse* and *Populations and Races*.

As Foucault's fame rose ever higher, he began to receive an overwhelming amount of correspondence and requests. Daniel Defert said in an interview:

> '*One can always recognize his typing. He didn't have anyone to type his texts. Only towards the end, from 1978, there was Françoise-Edmonde Morin who acted as his secretary at the Collège de France. There was so much mail that he couldn't reply, so he gave her the letters and told her roughly how to reply: "Say that I am ill"; she could even do a copy of his signature, which I can recognize.*' (Defert, quoted in Gordon, 2018)

The Fight Continues

Prior to the election of François Mitterand as President of France, Foucault's reputation had already been established on both the national and international stage. He had been ranked as France's third most influential intellectual, behind Claude Lévi-Strauss (1908–2009) and Raymond Aron (1905–1983) (Macey, 2019). The Mitterand government took up some of Foucault's suggested reforms to the criminal justice system, such as closing high-security wings in prisons, abolishing the death penalty and the state security courts. However, Foucault's engagement with the incoming administration was limited. He was not brought into government and declined an offer to become a cultural ambassador to New York.

Foucault continued to visit the USA during the early 1980s, travelling both to Berkeley, California, where he was appointed regent lecturer, as well as to New York. He gave interviews in New York in 1982 which discussed gay culture and sexuality. There had been increasing police pressure on S&M clubs and bathhouses in Toronto, Canada, which had led the authorities to close many establishments. In an interview with *Gai Pied*, he argued against the police's intolerance, so clearly on display. There should be, argued Foucault, intransigence about police intervention in sexual practices.

After a terrorist attack on Jo Goldenberg – a Jewish restaurant in Paris – in August 1982, Foucault committed to eating in the restaurant as a sign of resistance. Later that year, he published a book with the French historian Arlette Farge (1941–), examining the idea of 'disorderly families' in the 18th century. The book reproduced 94 letters of complaints, now held in the Bastille Archives, that had been written to the king of France requesting his intervention in family disputes. Farge and Foucault were fascinated by the way that the letters both illustrated and intervened in the workings of power and government process.

Failing Health

By late 1983, Foucault had begun to experience a series of illnesses, including persistent sinusitis. His doctors recommended several detailed pulmonary examinations in December and prescribed a course of antibiotics. He wrote to a friend, 'I thought I had AIDS, but an intensive treatment has set me back on my feet' (Defert, 2013). However, he visited the Tarnier Hospital, Paris, and it seemed that his main question was 'how much time do I have left?' (Defert, 2013). Despite this, in April 1984, he insisted on hosting a party at his home for the American novelist William Burroughs.

In early June 1984, Foucault suffered a series of health setbacks and was hospitalized at Saint-Michel Hospital, where he was placed in intensive care. Ten days later, while still in hospital, he received the third volume of his *History of Sexuality*. During his last days, doctors limited access 'because they were afraid to have anyone coming to the hospital – they were afraid of information getting out, quite simply' (Defert quoted in Gordon, 2018). In other words, there were concerns about rumors circulating in the press about Foucault's health. Foucault gave his last interview, just four weeks before his death, to writer Gilles Barbedette. Later, his friend Hervé Guibert (1955–91), a novelist and photographer, wrote a thinly disguised account of Foucault's last days in his book *To the Friend Who Did Not Save My Life* (1990). In it, he wrote about Foucault, using the name Muzil as a pseudonym. Writing about visiting the hospital on Foucault's last day, he wrote:

> *'when I walked down the corridor I saw that everyone had vanished, nobody was guarding the door, as though they'd all gone on holiday after a stretch of very hard work. I saw Muzil through the window once more under his white sheet, with his eyes closed and a tag tied around his wrist or maybe it was his leg, sticking out from under the sheet, and I could no longer enter*

that room, I could not kiss him anymore. I grabbed a nurse by her blouse and backed her out into the corridor, babbling, "It's true that he's dead? Is it? He's really dead?" (Guibert, 1995)

Foucault's final Will, written in 1982, included only a few recommendations. These included: 'death, not invalidism' and 'No posthumous publications'. In October 1982, Foucault told a freelance writer in Vermont, USA:

'I don't feel that it is necessary to know exactly who I am. The main interest in life and work is to become someone else that you were not in the beginning. If you knew when you began a book what you would say at the end, do you think you would have the courage to write it? What is true for writing and for a love relationship is true also for life. The game is worthwhile insofar as we don't know what will be the end.' (Martin et al, 1998)

Fig. 4 Grave of Michel Foucault (right), alongside the grave of his mother and father, at the cemetery of Vendeuvre-du-Poitou, north of Poitiers, France.

Michel Foucault's Timeline

Foucault	World Events

1923 Beginning of joint French and Belgian occupation of the German Ruhr

1926 Paul-Michel Foucault is born on 15 October

1934 Failed coup d'état instigated by far-right leagues in France; assassination of Chancellor Dollfuss by Austrian Nazis

1939 Outbreak of World War II: France declares war on Germany

1940 Sent to family house in Vendeuvre-du-Poitou during German invasion of France

1945 End of World War II

1945 Enters the Lycée Henri-VI in Paris

1945 Decolonization movement repressed in Algeria, resulting in 6,000 Algerians killed

1948 Obtains a BA in philosophy at the Sorbonne

1950 Joins the French Communist Party

1951 Treaty of Paris; establishment of the European Coal and Steel Community

1954 *Mental Illness and Personality* is published

1954 End of Indochina War leads to division of Vietnam

1957 Treaties of Rome; establishment of the European Economic Community and the European Atomic Energy Community

1961 Submits two doctoral theses at the Sorbonne	**1960** Decolonization of French Equatorial Africa and French West Africa
	1962 End of the Algerian War.
1963 *The Birth of the Clinic* and *Raymond Roussel* are published	
1966 *The Order of Things* is published; leaves Paris for Tunisia	
	1968 May '68 protests and strikes in France
1970 Elected as chair in the History of Systems of Thought at the Collège de France	**1970** Declaration of Mauritanian independence from France
1971 First lectures at the Collège de France and the creation of the Group for Information on the Prisons	
1975 *Discipline and Punish* is published	**1975** Decolonization of French Comoros after independence referendum
	1981 François Mitterrand elected French president
1983 Appointed regent lecturer at the University of California, Berkeley	
1984 Dies in Paris on 25 June of HIV-related illness	

2. Influences on Foucault's Thinking

Foucault's philosophy is anything but intimate, frequently taking an impersonal, objective style. In many ways, this fact makes his influences distinctly obscure. But let us suppose that there were three forms of influence on Foucault's philosophy. The first of these would be the questions that Foucault was drawn to and the political problems he posed. The second would be the crosscurrents of post-war European philosophy. The third would be the philosophical thought of intellectuals who preoccupied Foucault's life and works.

When seen together, these influences help us to understand Foucault's philosophy. And yet, in order to understand these influences, we need to see how they were made visible in his philosophical practice. This was unique: it used history to rethink philosophy, and philosophy to rethink history. As Foucault noted, this is a philosophy of diagnosis.

> *'Let's say I'm a diagnostician. I want to make a diagnosis and my work consists in revealing, through the incision of writing, something that might be the truth of what is dead [...] In that sense I would call myself a diagnostician. But is diagnosis the work of*

*the historian, of the philosopher, of someone involved
in politics? I don't know. In any event, it involves an
activity of language that is extremely profound for me.*
(Foucault, 2013)

While Foucault's diagnoses form part of his philosophical
project, his project also involved rejecting certain notions from
Western Enlightenment thought. For Foucault, it was necessary
to reject both humanism and an abstract, ahistorical idea of the
human subject. His project moved in another direction. He
placed the human subject within a network of relations between
laws, institutions, knowledge, practices and power. It is these
networks that, for Foucault, create the conditions for the human
subject and the possibility of life itself.

The Politics of Life

The principle question for Foucault centred around the history
and politics of the human subject. The 'politics of life' runs
throughout Foucault's philosophy, whether he is studying a
prisoner or someone within an insane asylum. His diagnoses of
the politics of life can be seen clearly across all of his activities,
from his political activism and interviews to his books, dossiers,
pamphlets and lectures at the Collège de France.

Foucault was at the centre of leftist politics before and after
the events of 'May '68', as this period has become known in
France, where student strikers were joined by a diverse mix of
union workers and activists of all ages and occupations. After the
fervour of 1960s radicalism, he was witness to the subsequent
state repression, criminalization and surveillance of protestors
and activists. In the 1970s and 1980s, we can see with hindsight

how he attempted to diagnose political developments and write a 'history of the present'. For Foucault, this was a historical present characterized by new forms of power and knowledge in prisons, the police, psychiatry, surveillance, punishment, neoliberalism and sexuality.

Foucault's thinking was also informed by his time living in Tunisia, where he taught philosophy at the University of Tunis for three years in the late 1960s. Here he was involved in anti-imperial, anti-authoritarian activism, a little over a decade after Tunisia had gained independence in 1956 from French colonial rule. Although Foucault is often associated with the political events of May '68 in France, he was not even in France at the time. Instead, Foucault said that his time in Tunisia was the catalyst for a profound change in his life and work. In an interview in 1978 with Duccio Trombadori, he said that 'Tunisia, for me, represented in some ways the chance to reinsert myself in the political debate.' (Foucault, 1991a)

It was in Tunisia that Foucault developed ideas for his book, *The Archaeology of Knowledge*, while speaking regularly at a cultural centre – Club Tahar Hadad – run by a feminist activist named Jellila Hafisa. This was a period in which student protests and civil unrest were directed towards the authoritarian government. Following the widespread arrest of student activists, Foucault invited protesters to use his apartment as an organizing space. He supported imprisoned activists' legal cases and compiled evidence for their defence. During this time, he began to develop a new understanding of the relation between power and protest, desire and repression. This led him to ask:

'What on earth is it that can set off in an individual the desire, the capacity, and the possibility of an absolute sacrifice without being able to recognize or suspect the slightest ambition or desire for power and profit? This is what I saw in Tunisia. The necessity for a struggle was clearly evident there on account of the intolerable nature of certain conditions produced by capitalism, colonialism and neo-colonialism.' (Foucault quoted in Medien, 2019)

Upon returning to Paris in 1968, Foucault's activism was marked by his involvement with several activist groups, including the *Group Information Asiles* (GIA) and *Group d'Information sur les Prisons* (GIP). Both of these groups supported inquiries led by patients and prisoners. The GIA posed political questions about the treatment of madness, mental illness, psychiatry and asylums.

In 1971, Foucault said that the GIA had 'already started interventions in the asylums, using methods similar to those employed in the prisons' (Elden, 2017). The group set out to challenge psychiatry and how it exercised power over patients and throughout society. It questioned the validity of the very foundations of psychiatry, and, like other anti-psychiatry movements in the period, claimed that 'psychiatry was an instrument of repression of the oppressed class' (Elden, 2017).

Foucault's involvement with the GIP began in 1971. In many ways, his political activities in this group are key to understanding the development of his ideas about power, punishment and the body. This was a group, he wrote, that 'focused on attacking the repressive system in the way it works in France and probably also in other countries' (Elden, 2017). Its aim was to collect and publicize information about prisons, not to propose prison reforms. The group was based on the principle that police control was tightening on a day-to-day basis, and that no one was certain of avoiding or escaping prison.

The GIP included the philosopher Hélène Cixous (1937–), the writer Jean Genet (1910–86), and Jean-Marie Domenach (1922–97), editor of *Esprit*. The founding manifesto was signed by all members of the group, and published in at least three places, including philosopher Jean-Paul Sartre's journal, *J'accuse*. It laid out the group's principle concern about increasing authoritarian control, and noted that:

> 'Little information is published on prisons. It is one of the hidden regions of our social system, one of the dark zones of our life. We have the right to know; we want to know. This is why, with magistrates, lawyers, journalists, doctors, psychologists, we have formed a Groupe d'Information sur les Prisons. We propose to make known what the prison is: who goes there, how and why they go there, what happens there, and what the life of the prisoners is, and that, equally, of the surveillance personnel [...] how one gets out and what it is to be, in our society, one of those who came out.'
> (Elden, 2019)

One of the aims of the group was to give a voice to prisoners. The group did this in several ways, including the use of questionnaires, making a film where prisoners spoke about their experiences, and by publicly highlighting hunger strikes within the prisons.

While the GIP allowed prisoners to speak for themselves, there was nevertheless a prominent role for intellectuals to guide and shape those voices. It would be naive to say that prisoners were 'set free' to voice their criticism of prisons. The intellectuals took a role in editing the accounts of prisoners and framed prisoners' testimonials within the group's broader agenda.

Throughout Foucault's activism in Tunisia, with the GIA and GIP, he encountered new and formative ideas. While working with the GIP, he discovered the Black Panthers' analysis of prisons and systemic oppression in the writings of American activists Angela Davis (1944–) and George Jackson (1941–71). This was important in developing his critical method, and allowed him to further examine oppressive power structures, as he came to understand that prisons were part of broader technologies of power.

European Philosophy in the 1950s and 1960s

In order to understand Foucault as a philosopher, it is necessary to put his work in the context of several philosophical movements that predominated Western European intellectual circles. While his career spanned university postings in Tunisia, France and the USA, he was a scholar whose ideas are most immediately relevant to post-war Western European (particularly French) philosophical thought. This was an intellectual context in which phenomenology (the study of the structures of experience and consciousness), structuralism (see Chapter 3), Freudianism and Marxism held predominant influence in philosophy and the human sciences. While his approach to philosophy differed from proponents of each of these approaches from the 1940s and 50s, they were the touchstones for many of his most forceful criticisms and interventions in philosophical debates during the 1960s and early 1970s.

In one sense, this was an intellectual context dominated by the existentialism, phenomenology and Marxism of Jean-Paul Sartre. From the 1940s, Sartre and other existentialists, such as Raymond Aron, Albert Camus (1913–60) and Simone de Beauvoir (1908–86), played a key role in translating and developing the phenomenological ideas of Søren Kierkegaard (1813–55), Edmund Husserl (1859–1938) and Martin Heidegger (1889–1976). As it became clear to Foucault, before and after his admission to study philosophy in Paris, the intellectual climate of post-war French philosophy was dominated by the phenomenological idea of a transcendental human subject.

This was an approach to philosophy that examined the human subject through detailed descriptions of the subjective perception of phenomena. This phenomenological tradition seeks to study consciousness as it is experienced by humans through the structures of perception, meaning and understanding that make sense of things in the world. According to phenomenologists such as Husserl and Heidegger, these 'structures of experience' can be studied and described through objective inquiry. Any phenomena outside of human consciousness were not of interest as objective things in the world; , phenomena (from a table to a thought) were studied as things only so much as they appeared in human experience. This was a study of consciousness and existence, founded on the notion of a transcendental subject who was a rational being. In many ways, this philosophy began and ended with the examination of human consciousness.

Phenomenology was based on the assumptions of European Enlightenment philosophers, such as Immanuel Kant (1724–1804), who believed that humankind's essence was its ability to think and reason. But Foucault saw another side to this Enlightenment belief in universal reason. The European Enlightenment had a hidden history of exclusion and confinement. Enlightenment philosophy and science had discovered a new problem with its belief in universal reason: if humankind's essence is its ability to reason and think, how should madness be understood? And, what should be done with the mad? Foucault came to find that Enlightenment philosophers thought that madness was an aberration that had to be explained, excluded and confined in asylums.

Foucault's philosophy rejected a philosophical tradition that examined phenomena and a transcendental, knowing subject. It denied a triumphant account of scientific progress. But in order to critique this philosophical tradition, he would need to draw on different types of philosophical thought. Foucault was drawn towards the works of relatively marginal philosophers in the intellectual life of 1950s France: the French philosopher George Canguilhem (1904–95) and the German philosopher Friedrich Nietzsche (1844–1900).

Canguilhem and the History of Sciences

George Canguilhem was one of the most prominent influences on Foucault's philosophy of scientific knowledge. Before the two had met, Foucault would have known of Canguilhem through his formidable reputation as a medically trained historian of science, teaching at the University of Strasbourg in the 1950s.

Canguilhem was known for his abrasiveness and harshness. He was one of Foucault's principal examiners for admission to the École Normal Supérieure.

By paying tribute to Canguilhem in 1970 as a 'model and support', Foucault acknowledged a debt to someone who never formally taught him. Canguilhem helped Foucault in the preparation of his book on the concept of 'the medical gaze', *The Birth of the Clinic* (1963). His broader impact on Foucault's thinking about the history of science is evident from the introduction that Foucault wrote to Canguilhem's *The Normal and the Pathological* (1966), in which he remarked on a crucial paradox in Canguilhem's writings:

> '*this man, whose work is austere, intentionally and carefully limited to a particular domain in the history of science [...] has somehow found himself present in discussions where he himself took care never to figure. But take away Canguilhem and you will no longer understand much about Althusser [...] you will no longer grasp what is specific to sociologists such as Bourdieu [...] you will miss an entire aspect of the theoretical work done by psychoanalysts, particularly by the followers of Lacan.*' (Foucault in Canguilhem, 1966)

Foucault was principally influenced by Canguilhem's radical rejection of 'progressivism' in science and knowledge. Canguilhem described how historians of science have tended to assume that there has been a progressive improvement of scientific thought over time. This assumes that scientific ideas pass from common use only once they have been superseded by a better, more accurate idea, which is, in turn, replaced by an even better idea. In this sense, new scientific methods are replacements for older methods, and each new method is seen as an improvement upon the previous. But Canguilhem claimed that the sciences do not change in that manner.

In Canguilhem's histories of the life sciences, Foucault found a number of methodological principles that he would come to incorporate in his own research on psychiatry, psychology and other forms of scientific knowledge. Writing in the introduction to *The Normal and the Pathological*, Foucault says that science does not remove errors from knowledge, either through improvements or 'breakthroughs' within a discipline. For Canguilhem, sciences are 'discontinuous'. They do not develop along neat lines, but through interruptions, new discoveries and new conceptual revolutions. Science continuously remakes its own history.

According to Foucault, the importance of Canguilhem for other historians of science is that he opens up the possibility of a new understanding of the relationship between truth and science. Instead of thinking that science discovers new truths, he argued that there are only new ways of speaking truthfully within scientific discourses. This means that, rather than there being a final point in which truth can be spoken, there are certain conditions placed upon how truth can be put/placed into discourse. There are rules for producing scientific truth. As Foucault writes: 'Error is not eliminated by the muffled force of a truth which gradually emerges from the shadow, but by the formation of a new way of "speaking true"' (Foucault in Canguilhem, 1966).

A second principle that Foucault found in Canguilhem's work is the relation between the historical circumstances in which the historian writes and the period under historical examination. Canguilhem argues that scientific truth within the historian's time should not have any influence on writing the history of science. Today's scientific truths should not be used to critique past scientific errors. As he wrote, 'the outdated past is still the past of an activity for which we have to retain the name scientific' (Miller, 2000). The historian of science should not retrospectively reappraise a scientific error by using contemporary standards of truth. Canguilhem believed that the philosopher of science should examine the process through which scientific claims were once accepted as truthful, in its historical context.

In Canguilhem, Foucault found a guide for an alternate foundation to examine scientific knowledge. In contrast to phenomenology and humanism, Canguilhem offered a different method with which to pose problems about the history of scientific knowledge. Rather than taking as his starting point the existence of a rational, transcendent human subject, and the meaning that that subject gives to experience, Canguilhem's philosophy is one that includes ideas of error, concept and the living being.

Nietzsche and the Will to Power

A second important influence on Foucault was Friedrich Nietzsche – a philosopher who has always divided opinion. Foucault was at the forefront of a general movement to reappraise Nietzsche's philosophy, in the face of many other philosophers' concern about his admiration for military men, his opinions of women, his fear, hatred, and his contemplation of pain. Foucault repeatedly returned to Nietzsche's writings throughout the 1960s and 1970s. In a letter in August 1967, he wrote:

'I'm getting to the bottom of Nietzsche. I think I am beginning to see why he has always fascinated me. An account of the form of the will to knowledge in European civilization, which has been ignored in favour of an analysis of the will to power.' (Defert, 2013)

By the early 1960s, the influence of Nietzsche in France was becoming increasingly notable. The publication of philosopher Gilles Deleuze's *Nietzsche and Philosophy* in 1962 marked a renewed interest in his ideas among a burgeoning set of European philosophers. Deleuze claimed that Nietzsche was the true inventor of critical philosophy, because he offered a vociferous form of critique. This was not just the questioning of values, but the questioning of the value of values. It involved examining the value of both truth and knowledge. Foucault aligned himself with this philosophical tradition.

For Nietzsche, 'knowledge' is not the same as 'truth', nor is it reducible to the status of a belief. Rather, as Foucault wrote: 'Nietzsche said that truth was the most profound lie' (1991b). Knowledge has little to do with truth. All human knowledge is an invention and is grounded in historical and social circumstances. Knowledge is formed through techniques, technologies, practices and language. Nietzsche saw truth as tied to humankind's driving force and a 'will to power'. Truth is only one byproduct of this drive. For Nietzsche, as for Foucault, knowledge and truth is conditional on antagonism and the exercise of power.

When describing his interest in Nietzsche, Foucault remarked on his unique approach to philosophy. This was also a philosophy of diagnosis:

'I think that my continued interest in Nietzsche, the fact that I've never been able to position him absolutely as an object we can talk about, that I've always tried to frame my writing in relation to this slightly timeless, important, paternal figure of Nietzsche, is very closely related to this: for Nietzsche, philosophy was above all else a diagnosis, it had to do with man to the extent that he was sick.' (Foucault, 2013a)

What preoccupied Foucault about Nietzsche was the possibility that philosophy could be more than amusement, reflection or idle contemplation. Philosophy could be used for examination and treatment. As he stated, 'it was both a diagnosis and a kind of violent therapy for the diseases of culture' (Foucault, 2013a).

When Foucault was appointed chair in the History of Systems of Thought at the Collège de France, his inaugural lecture focused on Nietzsche and the will to power. And as Foucault began to develop ideas about the relation between power and knowledge, less as an intellectual exercise and more as a political struggle, he examined knowledge as a product of conflict. He realized that knowledge is not adjudicated through disinterested, idle reason, but through battles and skirmishes.

Deleuze and a New Ethics

The third notable influence on Foucault's philosophy was Gilles Deleuze. After publishing *Nietzsche and Philosophy* in 1962, Deleuze continued to write about other philosophers, such as Baruch Spinoza (1632–77) and Henri Bergson (1859–1941), as well as novelists such as Marcel Proust (1871–1922) and Leopold von Sacher-Masoch (1836–95) – the latter giving rise to the term 'masochism' (much to his displeasure), relating to his fondness for having women beat and whip him.

In February of 1962, Foucault became acquainted with Gilles Deleuze. There was an obvious ongoing affinity between them, displayed by their continued dialogue and collaboration. Foucault wrote that 'Perhaps one day this century will be Deleuzian'. Deleuze (1988) wrote that, with Foucault, 'A new archivist has been appointed'. Both authors expressed an interest in the role of intellectuals and power. During a discussion on these themes, Foucault set out his views on philosophical practice as a struggle against power, not for self-realization.

> ***Michel Foucault:*** *'A struggle against power, a struggle to bring power to light and open it up wherever it is most invisible and insidious. Not a struggle for some "insight" or "realization" (for a long time now consciousness as knowledge has been acquired by the masses, and consciousness as subjectivity has been taken, occupied by the bourgeoisie) – but a struggle to undermine and take power side by side with those who are fighting, and not off to the side trying to enlighten them. A "theory" is the regional system of this struggle.'*

> ***Gilles Deleuze:*** *'Yes, that's what a theory is, exactly like a tool box. It has nothing to do with the signifier [...] A theory has to be used, it has to work. And not just for herself. If there is no one to use it, starting with the theorist himself who, as soon as he uses it ceases to be a theorist, then a theory is worthless, or its time has not yet arrived.'* (Deleuze, 2004)

Both Foucault and Deleuze put these ideas into practice in shared political struggles. They collaborated on a pamphlet titled '*Intolérable*' for the GIP, in which Deleuze contributed an article on suicide. In December 1972 they set up the *Association de Défense des Droits des Détenus* (Association for the Defence of the Rights of Inmates). They also undertook collaborative work that examined 'equipments of power' such as urban infrastructures and public utilities.

It was Deleuze's collaboration with psychiatrist and philosopher Felix Guattari (1930–92) that made one of the most significant intellectual impacts on Foucault. After the publication of their book, *Anti-Oedipus: Capitalism and Schizophrenia* (1972), Foucault joked with Deleuze that now 'We have to get rid of Freudo-Marxism'. To which Deleuze was said to reply, 'I'm taking care of Freud, will you deal with Marx?' (Defert, 2013). In his preface to *Anti-Oedipus*, Foucault states that the book should not be read as a theoretical reference, but 'can best be read as an "art"' (Deleuze and Guattari, 1972). Following Nietzsche, this was a philosophical work that linked desire with power. It did this through the invention of new philosophical concepts, such as multiplicities, networks, and machines.

Foucault's thoughts on power were influenced by Deleuze's concept of capitalist 'machines' and what they could produce. Deleuze used the idea of machines to describe the manner in which political realities are actualized. His machines are entities that bring about political changes. Foucault took up these ideas, notably in his examination of prisons and disciplinary power, examining how these machines 'seek connections' to other machines and how bodies are subject to the controls exerted by those machines.

Foucault said that Deleuze and Guattari's *Anti-Oedipus* also proposed a new form of ethics. It was, he wrote, 'the first book of ethics to be written in France in quite a long time' (Foucault, 2013c). This is an ethics of being 'anti-Oedipal'. And what is this ethic? Foucault summarized some of the maxims that he found in this work:

> • *'Free political action from all unitary and totalizing paranoia.'*
>
> • *'Withdraw allegiance from the old categories of the Negative (law, limit, castration, lack, lacuna), which Western thought has so long held sacred as a form of power and an access to reality.'*
>
> • *'Do not think that one has to be sad in order to be militant, even though the thing one is fighting is abominable.'*
>
> • *'Do not become enamoured of power.'* (Foucault, 2013c)

For Foucault, these are maxims for everyday life and combine to form an ethic which breaks out of the confines of Freudian and Marxist thought. The two philosophers would continue to debate and inform each other's philosophical practice throughout their lifetimes, with Deleuze criticizing Foucault's notion that 'pleasure' was a concept of resistance (Gilliam, 2018).

Each of these three forms of influences – the political, philosophical, and intellectual – offer starting points to better understand Foucault's philosophical practice. And what is this philosophical practice? It is often remarked that Foucault presents a cynical vision of humans trapped, confined and powerless.

These are humans trapped within the prison of language, within systems of control, or within their bodies.

Also running throughout Foucault's philosophy is a radical critique of the human subject. Is the human being a reasoning subject? A criminal subject? A sexual subject? Foucault takes up the notion, borrowing from Canguilhem, Nietzsche, and Deleuze, that the human is the product of a historical relationship between knowledge and power. Throughout the next three chapters, we will show how Foucault examined these relations in terms of the birth of the human sciences, technologies of power, and practices of the self.

3. Birth of the Human Sciences

From the 17th century, the European Enlightenment prioritized scientific knowledge over dogma and received wisdom. By the mid-20th century, there was a strongly held belief in the objective status of knowledge produced by the human sciences. Today, we find triumphant claims of new sciences of the human, such as behavioural economics, neuropsychiatry and digital sociology, which offer new scientific insights into the functioning of humans' mental and social lives. These human sciences only became possible after foundational transformations in Western thought.

During the 1960s, Foucault examined how philosophers and scientists began to treat humans and human populations as objects of scientific inquiry. What is new about these sciences, said Foucault, is the manner in which they treat humankind as an 'empirical entity' (Foucault, 2004). Prior to the Enlightenment, he said, the topic of 'the human' was not a problem for scientific knowledge. But what is the difference, he asked, between the modern human sciences and non-scientific knowledge about humans? What is it that makes particular forms of information about humans into a 'science'? When and how did these sciences emerge? And how did these sciences produce knowledge about human populations? To answer these questions, Foucault examined several sciences of man, including economics, psychology and linguistics.

For Foucault, each of these sciences raise important issues about how scientific knowledge is established, what counts as truth and falsity in the human sciences, and how scientific knowledge is represented through language. He argued that we are in a historical era where human sciences are essentially concerned with the 'unveiling of the non-conscious' (Foucault, 2001). In order to understand how these sciences emerged from the 18th century, we need to explain how Foucault proposed to analyze the *discourses* of these sciences. After we have explained his ideas of *discourse* and *episteme*, we will go on to examine the birth of the human sciences, using economics as an example.

The Discourse of Scientific Knowledge

Foucault used the concept of discourse to begin his analysis of scientific knowledge. In his philosophy, 'discourse' refers to the language practices and signs that constitute knowledge. These practices are the possible methods of speaking and writing for people in any culture or time. Foucault borrowed and adapted this concept from the French structuralist linguists, such as Ferdinand de Saussure (1857–1913), who used it to examine the rules that organize a language. For the structuralists, an individual sign holds a specific meaning only through its relation to other signs. For example, any single word attains meaning only by its relation to other words within a sentence. As Pettit (1975) explains, the word 'flow' for instance, may be related to 'river', 'time' or 'thought'; it may be connected with various adverbs (such as 'quickly' or 'smoothly');

and it relates to other words with similar connections, such as 'flees', 'moves' and 'runs'. If a word loses some of these relationships over time, it loses 'its old formal identity' (Pettit, 1975). If 'flee' no longer exists, 'flow' changes subtly in meaning. This network of interrelated signs constitutes a discourse. What is important for the structuralists is that meaning is constructed through sequences and networks of signs (such as words).

Foucault used this concept to examine how the discourses of the human sciences are ordered. He examined the emergence of these sciences through their archives, focusing on large numbers of published materials in specific historical periods. These archives contain a system of signs about these sciences that can be analyzed to reveal how scientific discourses are structured, and the set of rules and practices that were used within that discourse.

Foucault turned to these archives with a method that he called 'archaeology'. This method involved the diagnosis of long-term changes within a discourse. Foucault did not regard this method as a science 'or even the beginnings of a future science' (Foucault, 1992), but it allowed him to examine the systematic rules with which individual statements relate to one another within a discourse. It is, he wrote, 'a possible line of attack for the analysis of verbal performances' (Foucault, 1992).

From Foucault's perspective, discourses should not be analyzed with reference to a 'speaking subject'. In other words, we should not think of discourse as owned or created by particular individuals. Foucault believed that individuals are only able to make truthful statements by adhering to the rules of that discourse. He suggested that through an archaeology of discourses, 'one could draw up a specific description of statements, of their formation, and of the regularities proper to discourse' (Foucault, 1992). He said that the human sciences 'constitute and establish their norms' in discourse. It is only because of those regularities – their established norms, rules and practices of speaking – that scientific knowledge can be produced.

With this archaeological method, Foucault wrote a history of the human sciences as 'science-objects' (Foucault, 1992). His method of analysis is principally an exploration of the rules and practices of a particular discourse. It is focused on the language used by these sciences, rather than analyzing, for example, the practical work of scientists, how they conduct experiments or collect observations. Foucault used his archaeological method to describe the rules of the human sciences, most notably in three publications during the 1960s.

In *Madness and Civilization*, Foucault described scientific knowledge of 'madness', and a series of concepts in psychiatric discourse. In *The Birth of the Clinic*, he examined how medical discourse changed in the 19th century. Foucault described this book as a series of 'out-takes' (Defert, 2013) from his earlier work (Madness and Civilization). Lastly, he turned to the sciences of life, labour and language in *The Order of Things* by examining the emergence of the human sciences that supplanted General Grammar, Natural History, and the Analysis of Wealth. Let us look a little more deeply at his ideas to better understand what Foucault can teach us about the human sciences.

The Order of Things

In *The Order of Things: An Archaeology of the Human Sciences*, Foucault introduced an important concept that we need in order to understand the emergence of the human sciences: episteme. Foucault adapted this concept from the Greek word for knowledge: *epistēmē*. In Foucault's usage, episteme is a historically specific set of conditions for knowledge; the manner of thinking that is unique to each historical era. Each era has its own episteme, making different kinds of distinctions between true and false statements and different rules for structuring knowledge. In any given culture and at any given moment, there is always only one episteme that defines the conditions of possibility of all knowledge, whether expressed in a theory or silently invested in a practice (Foucault, 2001).

Importantly, our current era is the Modern era, so we are living in the Modern episteme. Foucault said that the Modern episteme 'still serves as the positive ground of our knowledge' (Foucault, 2004). It was only at the start of this episteme that the human sciences became possible. Prior to that, Foucault says, the human did not exist as an object for scientific knowledge. In making this claim, Foucault suggests that discussion of the 'great advances' of contemporary human sciences fails to acknowledge that we still operate within the same historical era as 18th-century scientists.

At the start of *The Order of Things*, Foucault describes a painting by the 16th-century Spanish artist, Diego Velasquez. This painting marked a transition to a new painterly practice for representing the human. When speaking about the inception of his book, Foucault explained how his ideas came to him while studying this painting.

> *[O]ne day in Madrid, I had been fascinated by Velazquez's Las Meninas. I'd been looking at the*

painting for a long time, just like that, without thinking about talking about it someday, much less of describing it – which at the time would have seemed derisive and ridiculous. And then one day, I don't recall how, without having looked at it since, without even having looked at a reproduction, I had this urge to write about the painting from memory, to describe what was in it. As soon as I tried to describe it, a certain colouration of language, a certain rhythm, a certain form of analysis, especially, gave me the impression, the near certainty – false, perhaps – that I had found exactly the right language by which the distance between ourselves and the Classical philosophy of representation and Classical ideas of order and resemblance could come into focus and be evaluated.' (Foucault, 1966)

As Foucault said, this is how he began to prepare his book, *The Order of Things*.

'For that book I used material I had gathered in the preceding years almost at random, without knowing what I would do with it, with no certainty about the possibility of ever writing an essay. In a way it was like examining a kind of inert material, an abandoned garden of some sort, an unusable expanse, which I surveyed the way I imagine the sculptor of old, the sculptor of the 17th or 18th century, might contemplate, might touch the block of marble he didn't yet know what to do with.' (Foucault, 2013a)

Foucault used the insights he gained from this painting to depict the transformation of knowledge in the 17th and 18th centuries. This marked the beginning of a new manner of representation, which marked a shift in perspective – the beginning of a different discourse had arisen during the Modern era.

Fig. 5 *Las Meninas* painted by Diego Velàzquez in 1656.

Natural history had become 'biology'; the analysis of wealth had become 'economics'; reflection upon language had become 'philology'; and classical discourse – in which being and representation found its common locus – had been eclipsed. In the profound upheaval of such an archaeological mutation, Foucault said, the human being appears in the ambiguous position as both an object of knowledge and as a subject that knows (2001).

The scientist Thomas Kuhn (1922–1996) had claimed in his book, *The Structure of Scientific Revolutions* (1962), that science evolved not by linear progression but by leaps between paradigms, as the entire structure of understanding for one or another science was replaced by a new perspective in every era. This was due to 'revolutionary' discoveries that spin us into a completely different way of seeing things. Kuhn claimed that it is this new perspective that allows for a different understanding and knowledge of things. Foucault took this further; where Kuhn suggested the existence of multiple paradigms (at least one for each scientific field), Foucault makes a grand, albeit dubious, claim that only one episteme underlying the whole of a culture exists in each historical era. Notably, Foucault focused his analysis on scientific knowledge in European societies only, neglecting other geographical settings and other ways of thinking, which would display different epistemes. And, in fact, at times his definition of episteme does seem to allow for multiple, overlapping epistemes to exist within European societies.

Foucault acknowledged that there is more than one way of thinking in any one historical period. But he focused on the one particular episteme that he knew best – the human sciences in Europe – to show that those human sciences were made possible through a distinct arrangement of language and discourse. These arrangements are the only things that make it possible to distinguish truth from error, draw up categories of knowledge and evidence, and deliver a representation of knowledge within the human sciences.

Classical and Modern Epistemes

In order to understand the emergence of the human sciences, we need to understand what changed between the Classical and the Modern epistemes – in the paradigm shift between the Classical and the Modern era. In the most basic terms, the Classical episteme created knowledge through the ordering of objects, beginning with Aristotle's classification of animals into genera and species. For the sciences of the Classical episteme, Foucault argues, knowledge was created through an 'exhaustive ordering of the world' (Foucault, 2001).

The Classical age created this order through inventing new taxonomies of objects and living things. For example, taxonomies were used to distinguish varieties of species according to their particular characteristics (such as having feathers). This order was produced through an analysis of how much one thing – a language or a species – resembled another. These similarities were often depicted through the use of tables and charts. As Foucault wrote: 'The centre of knowledge, in the 17th and 18th centuries, is the [mathematical/scientific] table. As for the great controversies that occupied men's minds, these are accommodated quite naturally in the folds of this organization.' (Foucault, 2001)

For example, in the Classical episteme, each living organism was seen as having its own place in a universal order. Knowledge about each organism was based on measuring its similarities and differences from other organisms and then cataloguing the differences between entities in voluminous versions of encyclopedias.

In the Modern episteme there was a new mode of representing the human which gave rise to the new empiricism of the human sciences (Foucault, 2001). One of the main characteristics of the Modern episteme is the integration of mathematics. Mathematics introduced a new hierarchy between different forms of scientific knowledge. Those sciences which used mathematics were now considered as more scientifically rigorous, and higher up in the hierarchy of sciences. This meant that the other (non-mathematical) sciences began to be considered less rigorous and scientific.

In *The Order of Things*, Foucault concentrated his analysis of the Modern episteme on three empirical sciences of the human: the studies of labour, life and language. These sciences emerge from, and traverse, what Foucault calls the 'epistemological field' and they redefined the set of scientific laws that govern human conduct. Each of these domains are predicated on the fact that humans are 'unconscious' of the forces that govern their life, labour and language. But, importantly, Foucault realized that humans do not need to be consciously aware of the rules that govern their behaviour. For example, when we learn to talk we are unconscious of the rules that underpin the language that we are beginning to speak. Foucault is not referring here to grammatical rules, but everything about language, including what deserves a word, a label or a name.

Importantly, language itself becomes an object of scientific knowledge in the Modern episteme. Previously, language had been thought of as a 'transparent' tool with which to represent knowledge, but this gradually changed as it became recognized that language is both impure and imprecise. In evidence of this shift towards treating language as an object, Foucault points to the new sciences that began to interpret language, such as psychoanalysis and linguistics – those which sought to uncover hidden, unconscious structures.

Once language had been demoted 'to the mere status of an object' (Foucault, 2001), there was now value in studying the rules of language and the ways in which scientific knowledge uses language. This meant that sciences in the Modern episteme began to develop a new scientific use of languages through both the use of mathematics and a more formal system for describing phenomena.

The Sciences of Life, Labour and Language

Foucault said that a new form of scientific knowledge – the human sciences – began in the Modern era. This included biology (the science of life), economics (the science of finance and labour), and linguistics (the science of language). Foucault claimed that these sciences created a new relation between the human being and scientific knowledge. He described these human sciences as discovering, not what humans are by nature, but what a human *does* through its living, labouring, and speaking. He went so far as to say that, not only were there no human sciences before this point, but 'man did not exist (any more than life, or languages, or labour)' (Foucault, 2001). The Classical episteme could not conceive of the human being as an empirical object for scientific study. But in the Modern episteme, humankind is determined by historical, unconscious forces. These are the determining forces that set the conditions for human experience.

The emergence of the Modern episteme had important consequences for the organization of scientific knowledge. First, the human being became the foundation of all knowledge – because the human is the source of representation of the empirical world and reality. And yet, second, the human being is also 'present, in a new way that cannot even be termed privileged, in the element of empirical things' (Foucault, 2001). This was a historical event for the Modern episteme. As he writes,

> *'for the first time since human beings have existed and have lived together in societies, [the fact that Man] should have become the object of science – that cannot be considered or treated as a phenomenon of opinion: it is an event in the order of knowledge.'* (Foucault, 2001)

According to Foucault, these empirical sciences emerged at a historical conjuncture in the 17th and 18th centuries. They resulted from wider changes in language and discourse, which were brought about by problems with preceding forms of knowledge. For example, the birth of economics (as the science of finance and labour) only happened after philosophers recognized that the relationship between money and value was arbitrary.

At the same time, after the birth of the human sciences, there was a broader transformation of all scientific knowledge. In the Classical episteme, there was a clear ordering of knowledge. This was established through differences and placing different types of knowledge in an order. But in the Modern episteme, this order has become highly fragmented.

As Foucault wrote, there are complex relations between various forms of scientific knowledge, so much so that there is no clear order or distinction between them, as different sciences incorporate various forms of knowledge. According to Foucault, there are three dimensions of knowledge in the Modern episteme: formal knowledges (such as mathematics and physics); empirical sciences (such as biology, economics and philology, corresponding to the sciences of life, labour and language); and philosophical reflection. The human (empirical) sciences have fragmented relations with both formal knowledge (through the use of mathematical techniques, such as statistics) and philosophical reflection (through abstract theorization).

In this last section, we will follow Foucault's analysis of the birth of economics to further explain how the human sciences emerged in the Modern episteme. This will allow us to exemplify how economics emerged from the Classical episteme. Only once the concept of labour became a determining law within economic discourse could there be said to be a science of the economy.

The Birth of Economics

For Foucault, the emergence of economics as a science was only possible after the discovery of labour as a determining law. The science of economics began with a simple problem: how should a science examine humans through the objects they make and economic activity? So, for example, how should economics examine the production of pins, paper or books? For Foucault, it was only after the discourse of economics discovered the concept of 'labour' that it could begin a scientific analysis of norms, rules, patterns and associations. This was the main discovery of the two most important economists in the 18th century: the Scotsman Adam Smith (1723–90) and the Englishman David Ricardo (1772–1823).

Foucault wrote that economics is a science that enables humans to know 'in what the essence of labour and its laws consist' (2001). Previously, there had been no essences in economic knowledge. There had been no concepts which played an absolute, determining force. In the Classical episteme, Foucault writes, the economy had no causality that was particular to itself. This is due to the fact that there was no concept of economic production.

As such, Foucault explained, there was no science of economics and no political economy in the Renaissance or the Classical episteme. In the Renaissance episteme, the concepts of money, price, value and markets were the key concepts in discourses about the economy. This discourse was focused on the analysis of wealth – which itself was primarily focused on money and how the price of commodities was represented by money. At the time, money had an intrinsic character that enabled the measurement and substitution of a commodity's value.

By the Classical period, the concept of exchange determined a commodity's value. Money enabled the representation of values: 'as a name represents an image or an idea, yet does not constitute it' (Foucault, 2001). Classical discourse on the economy conceived of 'wealth' through its representation by 'money', all in order for economic exchange to exist. However, the Classical episteme came to recognize that 'money' does not have an intrinsic value, because any object could function as a form of currency. Also, for the Classical discourse, the relation between wealth and money was based upon the necessity of exchange.

In the 18th century, a group of French thinkers who called themselves the Physiocrats founded the first systematic and 'scientific' study of economics. They introduced the notion that exchange is possible only when a person has an excess of something that another person needs. For example, when a farmer has surplus fruit, the surplus can be sold at market for money. Wealth, for the Physiocrats, was provided by nature only when it was relinquished for money.

For Foucault, the analysis of wealth in the Classical era existed through a finely balanced order of things in the world. This meant the objects, such as fruit, that were introduced into economic exchange had an equivalent value to other things in exchange (such as cattle food, or clothing). There was an accordance between different things, so one apple could be equivalent to four strawberries, for example. But this ordering of things underwent a transformation, Foucault says, after the introduction of the concept of labour into economic discourse.

Foucault argues that it was Adam Smith, the 18th-century Scottish philosopher, who founded modern economics. Labour, for Smith, was not dependent upon other things. Labour was an end in itself. It was, in short, a determining force for other concepts in economics, such as value and wealth. It can be a part of the equation, as they can. This is because labour

> '*is an absolute measure, if one takes that to mean that it is not dependent upon men's hearts, or upon their appetites, it is imposed upon them from outside: it is their time and their toil.*' (Foucault, 2001)

Humans exchange labour when they experience a need or a desire, but they also exchange this labour because needs and desires are subject to time and necessity (there are many things we need, and we do not have time to make them all). Smith saw that there are additional conditions which make it possible to undertake labouring activities: 'industrial progress, growing division of tasks, accumulation of capital, division of productive labour and non-productive labour' (Foucault, 2001). The introduction of the concept of 'labour' allowed economics to begin to analyze these norms and rules of labouring activities.

A second economist, David Ricardo, was also important for the development of economic discourse. In his book, *On the Principles of Political Economy and Taxation* (1817), Ricardo put forward the idea that labour is the 'source of all value'. Ricardo explained that it was the energy, toil, time and activity required in producing a commodity that lay at the origin of its value. Labour, rather than wealth or exchange, was now recognized as a determining force in economics.

Foucault saw that Smith and Ricardo made a substantive break within economic discourse, which 'explodes the unity of that notion' (Foucault, 2001). Contrary to popular opinion, it was not Marxist economics that made this break. Foucault claims that Marxist economics only operates within this already existing episteme. As Foucault wrote: 'Marxism exists in 19th-century thought like a fish in water, it is unable to breathe anywhere else' (Foucault, 2001). Marxism is situated – can only exist – within the new economic discourse introduced by Smith and Ricardo.

The Unveiling of the Non-conscious

In this chapter we have shown that Foucault challenged some important preconceptions about the origin of Modern empirical human sciences. He saw them as a relatively recent invention in thought and the result of a transition from the Classical to the Modern episteme. In the Modern episteme, the human sciences are unified by a simple notion: that humans are the source of representation about the world. For example, in economics, it is humans and their labour that determine a commodity's value.

Foucault also challenges the notion that radical sciences, such as Marxist economics, are able to exist outside of Modern economics discourse. This is a discourse that emerged in the 18th century alongside a broader set of transformations in the order of knowledge. So, for Foucault, the human sciences originated from a change in the structure of discourses. This change involved a new epistemic concern with 'scientific' knowledge of the historical, unconscious forces that determine the conditions for human existence. These are sciences that set out on an 'unveiling of the non-conscious' (Foucault, 1966). According to Foucault, we are still living with the human sciences that perform this unveiling.

4. Technologies of Power

Foucault is possibly best known for his ideas about power. These offer a challenge to political philosophies that view power as an inherently repressive force. Foucault argued that the philosophies of Marx, Hegel and Freud need to be replaced with a new theory of power – one that understands that power is exercised through technologies of production, force and control.

During the early 1970s, Foucault drew inspiration from the Black Panthers, an American political organization whose analysis of the prison system struck Foucault as being significantly different to others of the time. Their analysis, he said, was 'free of the Marxist theory of Society' (Defert, 2013). Following the ideas of the Black Panthers, Foucault claimed that the effect of power is not solely to inhibit or repress people.

> *'It seems to me that it is a methodological and a historical error to consider power as an essentially negative mechanism of repression whose principal function is to protect, pressure or reproduce the relations of production.'*
> (Foucault, 2016a)

Power is not held by single persons of authority. Nor is power simply the system of laws and rules. Instead, for Foucault, power can only operate (exist) through technologies and the 'networks, currents, relays, points of support, differences of potential that characterize a form of power' (Foucault, 2006b). Power functions in the Modern era through the surveillance of people's bodies. It draws from scientific knowledge, such as psychiatry, to make decisions about whether these individuals are 'normal' or 'abnormal'. In order to illustrate his analysis, Foucault examined how power operates in the penal system on both the bodies and the souls of its inhabitants.

The Eclipse of Sovereign Power

Foucault argued against a political philosophy that associated the concept of power with sovereign authority. This was an account of power developed by political philosophers, such as Thomas Hobbes (1588–1679), who thought that the sovereign was the main source of political power. Foucault saw this as a conception of power that focuses on the violence and ceremonies that display a sovereign's divine rights, and through spectacular 'forces', such as experienced through coronations, torture or wars.

For philosophers such as Hobbes, the source of a sovereign's power was divine and therefore absolute. This power allowed sovereigns to take possession of all life – human and non-human – through justifying its acts as being 'in defence of the state'. This was a form of power that privileged the sovereign's decision about an individual's life and death. This was a power that had the right to seize and claim domains, possessions, bodies and life.

In the introduction to a series of letters in the Bastille Archive, Foucault argued that an individual's relation to sovereign power could nevertheless take more ordinary forms. Even sovereign power, he said, operated through discourse. The commonplace can be told, described, observed, categorized and indexed only within a power relation that is haunted by the figure of the king – by his real power or by the spectre of his might. Hence the peculiar form of that discourse: it required a decorative or supplicating language (Foucault, 2019).

Since the 18th century, Foucault said, power has increasingly operated without the need for a sovereign. Since this form of sovereign power has now passed, it is necessary to create a new theory of power. We must separate sovereignty from our theories.

> *'What we need, however, is a political philosophy that isn't erected around the problem of sovereignty [...] We need to cut off the King's head: in political theory that has still to be done.'* (Foucault, 1980a)

In the modern world of democratic states and bureaucratic structures, power plays a more pervasive role in people's lives. Power is not held or owned by an individual – such as a king or queen – but instead functions through systems and technologies. This is a theory of power that has no need for the notion of a sovereign, nor can individuals be liberated from its clutches. Escape is virtually impossible. In Foucault's theory, power functions through surveillance and discipline. These are the technologies of power that became increasingly widespread during the 17th and 18th centuries. (It is worth noting, however, that the criminologist David Garland (1985) has shown that some of these techniques of disciplinary punishment appeared in England around 100 years later than Foucault claimed.)

The Archaeology of Power

Foucault suggested that we should examine the emergence of technologies of power from the 17th century. His analysis started from the premise that previous theories of power – even his own – failed to recognize that power does not solely rely upon either ideology or violence. Foucault's ideas about power focused on two issues. First, the contemporary situation within the French prison system and how its power functions through law and punishment. Second, how new technologies of power have spread throughout society since the 17th century.

When Foucault established the *Group d'Information sur les Prisons* (GIP) in the 1970s, he was joined by a group of activists who were committed to 'attacking the repressive system in the way it works in France and probably also in other countries' (Elden, 2017). The group started several inquiries about the functioning of penal institutions, the conditions in prisons, and what prisoners, their families and the prison guards thought about those conditions. They produced pamphlets, manuscripts and a film, each of which were intended to critique the contemporary prison system.

Through one of the members of GIP, the French novelist Jean Genet, Foucault became aware of the political theories of imprisoned members of the Black Panthers. GIP members made contact with the Black Panthers later that year, and they went to California to meet with imprisoned members, later returning to Paris with documents for Foucault. Brady Thomas Heiner (2007) has argued that only after Foucault encountered the Black Panthers' analysis of prisons and American racism, did he begin his own analysis of technologies of power.

In the last of Foucault's 'Punitive Society' lectures in 1973, he began to outline some of the features of his new theory of power. He did so by arguing that power does not have the following characteristics: power is not possessed or appropriated by specific individuals or groups; the origin of power is not the State, but elsewhere; power does not reinforce capitalist modes of production, as power can exist in non-capitalist societies; and, an analysis of power should focus not on ideology, but on knowledge.

Given that power should not be theorized using those starting points, Foucault instead began to examine what he called *disciplinary power*. This is a power that produces particular types of souls and bodies. It is a power that disciplines populations to be more productive, docile and controllable. It does this by instilling new habits throughout society. This is a power that operates through daily practices, punishment, education and training. And, most importantly, it relies upon an apparatus that is built for 'manufacturing disciplines, for imposing coercions, and for instilling habits' (Foucault, 2015). For Foucault, the archetypical example of this apparatus is the prison.

Discipline and Punish: The Birth of the Prison

Foucault's analysis of power culminated in the publication of *Surveiller et Punir: Naissance de la Prison* (Discipline and Punish) in 1975. In this book, Foucault describes how power operates to punish, train and control bodies in modern societies. He argues that the technology of power that is most prevalent in our society is *disciplinary power*. This is not a form of power that is exercised through death, violence or torture, but a power that is exercised through attention to the most minute of details: how a body sits, eats, talks, walks, thinks. It is a power that is exerted through continual surveillance of bodies in prisons, schools and the army.

Foucault described a set of techniques for exercising of power that have proliferated since the 18th century. Populations' bodies are increasingly trained, taught new habits and transformed. These techniques are not principally concerned with executions or driven through imprisonment. Nor are these techniques on display in ceremonies or specular torture. Instead, these techniques aim towards the improvement, enhancement and maximization of a body's capacities. These are techniques that seek to make bodies more efficient workers and docile subjects.

Foucault was also interested in how these techniques of power grew in importance during the 18th century due to new forms of scientific knowledge. With the birth of new human sciences, such as sciences focused on a public health, Foucault saw a new relationship between power and knowledge. Knowledge becomes a tool for exerting power in society. For example, many new branches of sciences emerged that developed novel techniques for measuring, assessing and intervening in a population's health. These sciences were taken up by governments in order to collect information about populations through surveys, medical records, and so on, and they have been used in the development of new techniques that aimed to intervene in a population's health, birth and death rates.

Foucault describes one of the new mechanisms in the relationship between power and knowledge: the administrative survey. In his 1973 'Punitive Society' lectures, Foucault described how the administrative survey became a technique of power used to reform prisoners in the criminal justice system. Foucault writes that, during the 17th and 18th centuries, the introduction of the administrative survey produced new forms of statistical knowledge. The survey itself required new, specialized techniques for the collation and production of knowledge.

The birth of the administrative survey made it possible for the state to produce knowledge for managing the state and its systems – such as tax, education and health. The survey enabled the state to examine matters of concern to the state, such as the wealth or health of the nation, through surveying and producing knowledge about populations. Today, we still see how surveys are used to measure whether, for instance, prisoners are becoming rehabilitated. For Foucault, the birth of the administrative survey was closely tied to new forms of exercising power over populations, both inside and outside of the prison system.

While the survey is one such technique for the exercise of power, a technology of power brings together many different techniques, forms of power and knowledge, as well as architectural and concrete structures. Foucault concentrated his analysis of power on one key architectural structure, called the 'panopticon'. He analyzed the panopticon to illustrate how power is exercised across society. This structure, Foucault argued, best represents how power operates in schools, hospitals and army barracks. And for Foucault, this particular architectural design for a building (that was never built), typifies how disciplinary power works within our society.

Jeremy Bentham's Panopticon

Modern disciplinary power requires techniques for its application. In order to illustrate his philosophy of power, Foucault described

Fig. 6 Plan for the panopticon prison, designed by English philosopher and social theorist, Jeremy Bentham in the 18th century.

the design of an 18th-century prison put forward by the English philosopher, jurist and social reformer, Jeremy Bentham (1748–1832). Foucault saw Bentham as responsible for inventing a 'technology of power designed to solve the problem of surveillance' (Foucault, 1980a).

When Foucault was trying to understand the development of clinical medicine in the second half of the 18th century, he came across Bentham's designs for the panopticon. The name is derived from the Greek word *panoptes*, meaning 'all seeing', because Bentham's design – which was proposed as a blueprint for hospitals, factories, schools and prisons – was designed to allow those in charge to see and control all the people within the institution. The design consists of a central watchtower surrounded by cells. A watchman sits in the watchtower, while the prisoners (or hospital patients, workers, schoolchildren) occupy the cells. The watchtower shines out with light, so the watchman can see everyone in the cells, while those in the cells are unable to see him. The people in the cells have to act under the supposition that they are always being watched.

Reading more from the archive in which he'd discovered Bentham's panopticon, Foucault found that a major problem in medical discourse in the 18th century was about how to surveil, or continuously see, bodies in hospitals. This led to new designs of hospital wards that designated specific places for individual patients, so that each individual could be kept under observation. Foucault came to understand that there was a similar concern in reforming both hospitals and prisons in the 18th and 19th centuries, and Bentham's design offered a solution.

> *'I noticed that all the great projects for reorganizing the prisons (which date, incidentally from a slightly later period, the first half of the 19th century) take up this same theme, but accompanied this time by the almost invariable reference to Bentham. There was scarcely a text or a proposal about the prisons which didn't mention Bentham's "device" – the "Panopticon".'*
> (Foucault, 1980a)

The architectural design of the Panopticon enabled constant observation and inspection of prisoners in their individualized cells. Foucault noted that 'By the effect of backlighting, one can observe from the tower, standing out precisely against the light, the small captive shadows in the cells of the periphery. They are like so many cages, so many small theatres, in which each actor is alone, perfectly individualized and constantly visible.' (Foucault 1991c)

Prisoners could not see the guards who were watching them, but they would be aware that they were being constantly observed. The walls on the sides of each cell would prevent them from seeing other inmates in adjacent cells. Aware of their visibility to the central tower, each prisoner would begin to discipline themselves so that they behave appropriately. Knowing that they are being watched, prisoners are induced to recognize themselves as they are seen by prison guards. Foucault writes: 'There is no need for arms, physical violence, material constraints. Just a gaze. An inspecting gaze – a gaze that each individual under its weight will end by interiorization to the point that he is his own overseer [...] A superb formula: power exercised continuously and for what turns out to be minimal cost.' (Foucault, 1980a) For Foucault, it is the design features of the panopticon that would enable the 'automatic functioning of power' (Foucault, 1991c). Power would not need to be exercised through either force or violence – it could be exerted through the very architecture of the prison.

Foucault used the idea of the panopticon to present a general theory about how power operates in modern societies. However, his use of the panopticon has led to criticism that he does not appreciate the purpose of Bentham's design. According to Bentham scholar Anne Brunon-Ernst, 'Bentham's idea was not to create a panoptic society, where nothing would escape the gaze of the omniscient ruler' (2012). She argued that such a purpose would contradict a fundamental principle in Bentham's utilitarian thought, which was 'to do no harm'. That may be the case, but for Foucault, the panopticon provided a key insight into a greater understanding of how disciplinary power operates. It focuses on the functioning of individual bodies.

The Micro-physics of Power

Foucault showed that power does not operate through grand displays. In modern societies, power operates through habits and the smallest of actions. It is a form of power that infiltrates into the very fabric of thought, action, and feeling, and focuses on the differences between correct and abnormal behaviour.

On the point of habitual behaviour, Foucault refers to the 19th-century sociologist Émile Durkheim (1858–1917). Foucault says that for Durkheim and other sociologists, 'society [...] is the system of the disciplines'. For Foucault, however, the emergence of a new science of society – sociology – fostered a new sense that 'habits' are the very essence of social life. As Foucault wrote: 'Durkheim will find in our habits the very sign of the social' (Foucault, 2015). Through the emergence of sociology in the late 18th century, its proponents equated 'the social' with the 'habits' of a society's members. These habits are instilled in people through their membership of schools, workplaces and prisons. Individuals are expected to practice the habits of these places in alignment with everyone else, and there is a moral order that dictates that failing to adhere to these habits is deviant.

At the same time as the emergence of sociology, disciplinary power began to focus on disciplining these habits so as to exert control over populations. In his 1973 lectures on 'Psychiatric Power', Foucault advanced two hypotheses about disciplinary power. First, he claimed that disciplinary power 'reaches the level of bodies and gets a hold on them, taking actions, behaviours, habits and words into account' (Foucault, 2006b). This form of power puts itself in close contact with the physical human body. As Foucault phrases it, disciplinary power is a 'synaptic contact of bodies-power'. It touches and acts upon bodies.

Foucault's second hypothesis is that disciplinary power has a history. There is a history about the origins of each of these techniques and how they have been deployed. For Foucault, this history shows that disciplinary power has long been used within other settings, such as monastic communities. Over time,

Foucault showed, these techniques began spreading to more and more social institutions. He suggested that disciplinary power was present in medieval societies, though it was not the dominant form of power (Foucault, 2006b). But by the 18th century, disciplinary power had become the predominant form of power in the modern world.

We should also note that Foucault's analysis of disciplinary power is not essentially about the state. It is not focused on the apparatuses that the state uses, for example, to disseminate the ideologies of the bourgeoise class. He argued against the idea that the state uses institutions, such as the media or education, to disseminate an ideology to a population. For Foucault, power does not seek to indoctrinate or delude populations to accept capitalist relations. Instead, he said that disciplinary power makes populations more productive and more docile; it takes hold of bodies to change its habits. These are disciplines that treat the body as a machine to be optimized – so it can be made more efficient, effective and powerful. For Foucault, disciplinary power works to 'generate forces' in individuals (Foucault, 1990a). The disciplines attempt to control every individual's body in regard to its rhythms, biological processes, movements, health and sexuality; they shape bodies into productive entities by intensifying their productive capacities.

Docile Bodies

Now that we know a little more about what disciplinary power aims to do, we need to understand more about how disciplinary power achieves this end. Foucault's philosophy of power shows that disciplinary power works by focusing on *details*. He wrote that disciplinary power is a 'political anatomy of detail' (Foucault, 1991c). It is a form of power that specifically assesses and examines the details of bodies. Historically speaking, he argued that the 17th century rediscovered the 'body as object and target of power' (Foucault, 1991c). This rediscovery relied upon the scientific examination of the human body. These examinations found that the body is mutable and could be transformed through regulation and exercise.

Disciplinary power targets the body to order it into an 'obedient body'. This requires transforming a body's gestures, movements, rhythms and actions. Foucault referred to techniques for how soldiers are trained to walk and how students are trained to sit on a chair in a classroom. The effect of focusing on the body is to constantly correct the body so that it takes on specified forms. For example, students should be trained not to slouch or lean back on a chair. This training is achieved through detailed rules of conduct and by instilling habits, whether these be for army recruits, school pupils, hospital patients, factory workers or prisoners.

The Three Axes of Disciplinary Power

Foucault claimed that there are three axes through which disciplinary power exerts itself on bodies: through the ordering of space; through the organization of time and activities; and through controlling the relation between different bodies.

The first of these axes – using disciplinary power to order space – is exerted by creating partitions and enclosures. Think of a prison cell. Each cell is uniform in shape and size and has a designated number and an identifiable inhabitant. A prisoner is isolated and separated from other prisoners. In a school, each pupil will have a table space assigned to them. Both the cell and the table are made available for inspection by prison guards or teachers. Each body can be located in space. They cannot go missing or become lost in a group. At any moment, a prisoner or a school child can be observed.

The second axis is the use of disciplinary power to order time, through the scheduling of organized activities. Time is ordered through schedules and timetables, which use units of time to designate specific activities. Each unit of time is precisely calculated down to the nearest minute and second. A timetable can be used to monitor whether an individual body has completed an assigned task or is in the appropriate location. For example, in a factory, there is constant supervision of the time it takes to complete a work task. Distractions and disturbances are dispensed with in favour of individuals being forced to make the most efficient use of time. Each gesture of a factory worker can be broken down, calculated, measured, all in order to increase efficiency.

The third axis is the use of disciplinary power to order collective forces, by controlling the relation between individual bodies. This allows the collective exertion of force by multiple bodies when acting in unison. It maximizes each body's productive value. Think of army units and the division of labour in factories. Each individual body, in its movements and actions, is just one part of a larger machine. Discipline requires the ordering of bodies through the meticulous coordination of multiple units and groupings. This requires a structure and ordering of activities through systems of command.

Given Foucault's examination of disciplinary power, there are several criticisms of his historical approach. One main criticism levelled at Foucault is his Eurocentrism. Simon Legg (2007) has argued that Foucault is effectively silent on how these technologies of power had been initially tested by imperial powers during the colonialism of Africa, Asia and the Americas.

Foucault did indicate that some of the early examples of disciplinary technologies can be found in Jesuit missions and 'so-called "communist" Guarani republics' in Paraguay (Foucault, 2006b). He also described the need for a more detailed study of how disciplinary techniques were 'applied and refined in the colonial populations' (Foucault, 2006b). However, it is also true that Foucault discusses the permanent supervision in colonized states as a 'permanent penal system' (Chang, 2014).

Criticism of Foucault's 'Disciplinary Power'

The French philosopher Gilles Deleuze extended Foucault's arguments about disciplinary power by showing how this power has been supplanted by 'societies of control'. Deleuze used this term to illustrate how *control* has replaced *discipline* as the dominant form of modern power. Deleuze challenged Foucault's philosophy of power by noting the rapid acceleration of information that circulates about populations. This circulation enables a more immediate and expansive regulation of bodies. Also, while Foucault used factories and prisons as examples to demonstrate disciplinary power, Deleuze turned to capitalist corporations as better models for illustrating power in control societies. Corporations use varied techniques to exercise power, such as bonuses, rivalry, perpetual training and marketing. As Deleuze describes,

> *'the corporation constantly presents the brashest*
> *rivalry as a healthy form of emulation, an excellent*
> *motivational force that opposes individuals against one*
> *another and runs through each, dividing each within.'*
> (Deleuze, 1992)

A second criticism levelled at Foucault's idea of disciplinary power has emerged with the passing of time and the increased importance of new technologies to the operation of power. We live in a world where new mobile and smart technologies have proliferated. These technologies have introduced new possibilities for surveillance and control. The masses of new information that are collected about populations – held in databases, files, protocols and algorithms – also allow for new forms of surveillance and control over populations. Think of the utilization of biometrics and tracking technologies built into everyday objects, such as mobile phones. As the urbanist Stephen Graham notes:

> *'These constitute a working background, a ubiquitous*
> *computerised matrix of ever more interlinked devices:*
> *ATM cards and financial databases; GPS transponders,*
> *bar codes, and chains of global satellites; radio-frequency*
> *chips and biometric identifiers; mobile computers,*
> *phones and e-commerce sites and an extending universe*
> *of sensors built into streets, homes, cars, infrastructures*
> *and even bodies.'* (Graham, 2007)

In this way, Graham says, an individual's movements between different spaces and sites (within towns, cities or countries) entails 'a parallel movement of what sociologists call the "data subject" or "statistical person" – the package of electronic tracks and histories amassed as a means of judging the individual's legitimacy, rights, profitability, security or degree of threat' (Graham, 2007).

There is no longer any need for an architectural structure such as a panopticon in order to discipline bodies. These new forms of surveillance enable the disciplining of populations with dizzying rapidity.

5. Practices of the Self

After his work on technologies of power, Foucault started to think about how individuals made themselves into ethical subjects during the different historical eras. With our contemporary preoccupation with self-help guides, mindfulness and self-awareness training, yoga and meditation retreats, we can see how the self and our identity continues to be a key matter of concern.

During the last decade of his life, Foucault developed several projects to examine how philosophers in different historical eras thought about ethics and the self. He came to recognize that ethics and truth-telling are closely related to the exertion of political forces. Foucault's writings in the late 1970s and 1980s were concerned with questions of ethical existence and how people's moral life is governed by the self and others.

As Foucault became more preoccupied with questions of ethics and selfhood, he began to ask how people use practices of the self to make themselves into ethical subjects. These are practices that people use in their everyday life to give their actions meaning and moral substance. In order to understand these issues, Foucault turned to the writings of Ancient Greek and early Christian philosophers to understand the history of these practices.

Ethics and Philosophical Existence

By the mid-1970s, Foucault's attention turned to studying what he called 'the philosophical arts of existence'. He sought to understand how *the self* and *the truth* were connected in the Modern age. Foucault saw practices for telling the truth about the self as having a distinct history. As he wrote, 'the Modern age of the history of truth begins when knowledge itself and knowledge alone gives access to the truth' (Foucault, 2005). He argued that the Ancient Greeks and Romans were not so concerned with the precept 'know yourself' (*gnothi sauton*) as they were with the more expansive 'take care of yourself' (*epimelesthai sautou*) (Foucault, 1988). We have been misled into thinking that 'knowledge of the self' was more important to ancient thinkers than 'care of our selves' (and especially our souls, as he illustrates with textual examples from Socrates and Epicurean philosophers).

There have been several reasons for this obscuration, according to Foucault.

> '*First, there has been a profound transformation in the moral principles of Western society. We find it difficult to base rigorous morality and austere principles on the precept that we should give ourselves more care than anything else in the world. We are more inclined to see taking care of ourselves as an immorality, as a means of escape from all possible rules.*' (Foucault, 1988)

In addition, Foucault goes on,

> '*We also inherit a secular tradition which respects external law as the basis for morality. How then can*

respect for the self be the basis for morality? We are the inheritors of a social morality which seeks the rules for acceptable behavior in relations with others [...] "Know thyself" has obscured "Take care of yourself" because our morality, a morality of asceticism, insists that the self is that which one can reject.' (Foucault, 1988)

Foucault believed that practices of the self are used to express thoughts, actions and feelings and, in this way, they are the making of ethical subjects. He described these practices as being:

'the procedures, which no doubt exist in every civilization, offered or prescribed to individuals in order to determine their identity, maintain it, or transform it in terms of a certain number of ends, through relations of self-mastery or self-knowledge.' (Foucault, 1988)

A person's ability to tell the truth about the self is related, for Foucault, to ethics. Just as ethical thought has a history, those practices that people use to make themselves into ethical subjects also have a history. Ethical codes are simply 'grids of intelligibility' that subjects use to interpret their actions.

In the writings of philosophers and physicians, Foucault found that the problem of ethics and morality took different forms in different historical eras. And so, the relation between ethics and self is a philosophical and a historical question. Practices of the self, he wrote,

'seem to me to be good witnesses for a major problem, which is the genealogy of the modern self. This genealogy has been my obsession for years because it is one of the

> *possible ways of getting rid of a traditional philosophy*
> *of the subject.'* (Foucault, 2007)

This is a traditional philosophy of the subject that was put forward by 20th-century philosophers, such as Edmund Husserl, but has a longer history in the works of the 17th-century Enlightenment philosopher, René Descartes. Foucault argued that in this traditional philosophy, 'knowledge of the self (the thinking subject) takes on an ever-increasing importance as the first step in the theory of knowledge' (Foucault, 1988). The prioritization of knowledge, from the Enlightenment onwards, coupled with the distortion of the ancient philosopher's admonition to take care of our self and soul (rather than only know it) has become part of the technologies of the self.

While studying the ancient texts, Foucault also came upon a letter from the Stoic Marcus Aurelius, written in 144–5 CE. Noting the writer's examination of his conscience at the end of the letter, Foucault sees that one of the changes between the Hellenistic period and later Christian practices was the need to place the stress on 'what you did, not what you thought' (Foucault, 1988). 'The examination of conscience begins with this letter writing' he goes on, 'it dates from the Christian era and focuses on the notion of the struggle of the soul'.

Foucault also notes that 'Christianity is not only a salvation religion, it is a confessional religion [...] It imposes very strict obligations of truth, dogma, and canon'. It imposes the 'duty to accept a set of obligations, to hold certain books as permanent truth, to accept authoritarian decisions in matters of truth.' (Foucault, 2007) In addition,

'Each person has the duty to know who he is, that is, to try to know what is happening inside him, to acknowledge faults, to recognize temptations, to locate desires, and everyone is obliged to disclose these things either to God or to others in the community and hence to bear public or private witness against oneself.'

Foucault recognizes one such practice – the confession – as re-emerging as a tool in psychoanalytic treatment. He also drew attention to the fact that one predominant topic of confession is sexuality and sexual acts.

The History of Sexuality

In *The History of Sexuality*, Foucault examined how sexuality was treated as an ethical problem in different historical eras. As French philosopher Maurice Blanchot (1907–2003) notes, Foucault examined how the Victorians put sexuality into discourse 'with the aim of mastering one's most precious truth' (Blanchot, 1987). The 'truth' here refers to the truth of sex and sexuality. Writing in an introduction to the memoirs of a 19th-century hermaphrodite, Foucault argued that the notion that people have a true self or a 'true sex' has not left us (Foucault, 1980b). And, for the Victorians, a key concern was how to find the truth of sexuality through discourse.

Foucault's four-volume work, *The History of Sexuality*, examined various discourses on sexuality and sexual ethics. In the second and third volumes, titled *The Use of Pleasure* and *The Care of the Self*, Foucault turned to the Ancient Greeks, Hellenistic philosophers and Christian writings from the first and fourth centuries to examine how sexuality has been treated as an ethical problem.

Foucault argued that these discourses have been instrumental in shaping our cultural understanding of sexuality. There is no essential, natural sexuality that exists outside of history or discourse. We use discourses to think and talk about sexuality – our ideas about sexuality can only arise within the frame of our particular time, place and culture. These discourses also shape the relation between sexuality and ethics. Considering the fact that Foucault wrote a history of sexuality, it is ironic that he was not altogether interested in writing about sex. As he said in an interview: 'I must confess that I am much more interested in problems about techniques of the self and things like that than sex […] Sex is boring' (Foucault, 1997). Instead, discourses on sex, as found in philosophical treatises and texts by physicians, relate sexuality to health, the ordering of the home, friendship, economics and speaking truthfully.

Foucault's *The History of Sexuality* is mainly concerned with discourses about sexuality that treat it as an ethical problem. Another theme within this history is how practices of the self are used by people to discover truths about themselves. Throughout the four volumes, Foucault examines several practices of the self, such as the Christian Confession, dream interpretation, meditation, and the use of common-place books and journals. Through each of these practices, Foucault was interested in examining how the subject came to know and observe the 'truth' of their sexuality as a component of their ethical life.

These practices – sometimes called 'techniques' or 'technologies' – were of interest to Foucault because they allow people to reflect on their sexual and ethical lives and, crucially, because they allow people to govern themselves. For Foucault, people come to govern themselves through discovering the truth about their selves. On this point, Foucault wrote:

> 'Maybe our problem now is to discover that the self
> is nothing else than the historical correlation of the
> technology built into our history. Maybe the problem is
> to change those technologies [...] And in this case, one
> of the main political problems nowadays would be, in
> the strict sense of the word, the politics of ourselves.'
> (Foucault, 2007)

The notion of practices of the self should be seen as a development of Foucault's earlier work of discourse, knowledge and power. The previous chapter showed some of the ways that discipline is applied to subjects in prisons and other institutions. With this notion of practices of the self, Foucault also showed that these practices of the self are used by persons to govern themselves, not just through external controls, but through producing truths about themselves.

Through 'discovering' truths about ourselves, in ways such as working out what our dreams mean, we can come to a new understanding about how our actions have an ethical value. The dream experience cannot be isolated from its ethical content, he believed, 'not because it may uncover secret inclinations, inadmissible desires, not because it may release the whole flock of instincts' but because 'it restores the movement of freedom in its authentic meaning, showing how it establishes itself or alienates itself, how it constitutes itself as radical responsibility in the world' (Foucault, 1984–1985). As such, Foucault's examination of the self and subjectivity is related to both truth and knowledge.

In order to understand how these practices of the self operate, we should think of them as 'truth activities'. These practices allow subjects to speak the truth about themselves. People need practices and techniques to discover and speak this truth.

As we will go on to discuss in further detail later in the chapter, a prime example of such a practice is the Christian Confession. This is a practice that allows the subject to speak the truth about their actions to another person, who listens, interprets and guides a person's thoughts about those actions. Foucault did not argue that these practices function through repression. Quite the opposite. With confession, people are asked to speak honestly and openly to reveal their truth.

A History of Truth-telling

Foucault was concerned with comprehensively examining truth-telling practices and the constitution of the modern subject. He said that it is a historical problem to 'know how in a given society the individual binds himself to his own truth' (Foucault, 2014). In order to find a solution to this historical problem, he presents his project as an 'entire ethnology of truth-telling' (Foucault, 2014). Ethnology is traditionally understood as the study of different peoples and cultural practices. We need to understand a bit more about how Foucault thought about truth-telling before we examine the examples of avowal and the Christian Confession.

Instead of arguing that there has been one procedure through which truth is produced, the aim of Foucault's work during the 1970s and 1980s was to examine various practices that people use for telling the truth. He stated:

'the problem is that of knowing not under what conditions a statement is true, but rather what are the different games of truth and falsehood that are established, and according to what forms they are established.' (Foucault, 2014)

By examining these 'games of truth and falsehood', Foucault took it for granted that games have rules, tactics, strategies, and ways of being played, but each game is distinct. When Foucault talked about these different games, he understood that they have different rules in the human and natural sciences, but also in politics and government, the courts and the economy, and other settings. At the same time, Foucault argued, there is a societal obsession with inciting individuals to tell the truth about themselves, regardless of what settings they find themselves in. People are required, and can be punished for failing, to tell the truth about themselves. It is one of our primary social duties.

Foucault expanded upon these arguments in *The History of Sexuality*, mainly in Volume I, *The Will to Knowledge*. Here Foucault argues against the idea that there was a taboo on speaking about sex during the 18th and 19th centuries. There has been a popular myth, he says (which he calls the 'repressive hypothesis'), that Victorian morality led to a widespread censorship of discourse on sexuality. Writing in 1963, he argued that this hypothesis has been a popular, yet false, belief. Summing up Foucault's position, author David Macey writes:

'We readily believe that, in contemporary experience, sexuality has found once more a natural truth which supposedly waited for a long time in the shadows, under

*various disguises, before it had the right to come at last
into the full light of language, and which our positive
perspicacity now allows us to decipher.'* (Macey, 2019)

The myth of a repressive hypothesis has sustained the idea that
sex is a taboo topic, that desire and sexual acts are hidden away,
and that sexuality needs to be liberated. Foucault argued that this
is incorrect – neither sex nor sexuality has been repressed – and
instead draws attention to the proliferation of discourses about
sex since the 18th century.

One strong piece of evidence in support of Foucault's argument
is the emergence of new sciences that examine sexual behaviour and
desires, such as psychoanalysis. For Foucault, these new sciences
– which he calls *scientia sexualis* – led to a wide proliferation of
knowledge and discourse about sex. Indeed, sexuality has been a
major preoccupation of medical knowledge and literature, studies
of reproductive health and fertility rates, since the 19th century.

Foucault also argued that these sciences required procedures and
rituals for testing, observing, and demonstrating sexuality. One
of these procedures was adapted from the practice of Christian
Confession. Foucault identified how the practice of compelling
people to talk about sexual acts was taken up by scientists in the
19th century. And yet, this practice has a history dating back to
Christian monastic communities in the Middle Ages. During the
Counter Reformation, the practice of confession was increased
in Catholic countries and, Foucault notes,

*'it attributed more and more importance in penance
[...] to all the insinuations of the flesh: thoughts,
desires, voluptuous imaginings, delectations, combined*

movements of the body and soul; henceforth all this had to enter, in detail, into the process of confession and guidance.' (Foucault, 1976)

He continues,

'Sex was taken charge of, tracked down as it were, by a discourse that aimed to allow it no obscurity, no respite. This scheme for transforming sex into discourse had been devised [...] in an ascetic and monastic setting. The 17th century made it into a rule for everyone.'

In the 18th century, 'there emerged a political, economic, and technical incitement to talk about sex' (Foucault, 1976). This need to take sex 'into account', Foucault continues, derived not from a sense of morality but from the need to 'pronounce a discourse on sex that would derive [...] from rationality as well'. This idea was so shocking at first, he notes, that philosophers wondered, 'How could a discourse based on reason speak of *that?*' As philosophers struggled to direct their gaze 'to these objects situated between disgust and ridicule' they sought to avoid 'both hypocrisy and scandal'. It took the medical establishment another 100 years, he continues, to find a way to include sex within their discourse:

'One had to speak of it as of a thing not simply condemned or tolerated but managed, inserted into systems of utility, regulated for the greater good of all, made to function according to an optimum. Sex was not something one simply judged; it was a thing one administered [...] it had to be taken charge of by analytical discourses.'
(Foucault, 1976)

In this way Foucault shows that it was only after the adoption of confessional practice into modern sciences, and the incitement of people to talk about their sexual acts, that a rational approach was founded. This led to the sense that sex should be 'managed' and finally, a *scientia sexualis* arose, that claimed it held scientific knowledge about sexuality.

Before we examine the history of the Christian Confession, let us slow down and understand what Foucault meant by 'truth telling' and the act of *avowal*. By understanding the practice of avowal, we will be in a better position to understand how, for Foucault, practices of the self produce both truth and ethical existence.

The Truth of the Self

For Foucault, an essential part of the constitution of an ethical subject (how 'I' come into being as an ethical subject with agency) is the relation between speech and truth. Foucault examined a type of truth-telling practice that he calls 'veridiction'. This term is a neologism (newly coined word) formed from the Latin root *ver-*, meaning 'for truth', and -*diction*, meaning speaking, pronouncing, or telling. Through these veridiction practices, a subject (person with agency) produces a 'self' through their discourse. For law professors Fabienne Bion and Bernard Hardcourt, Foucault's interest in truth and 'truthful speech' is

> '*not a question of trying to determine the conditions that any assertion must fulfil to count as either true or false, but rather of analyzing the relation between truth games and games of power, where truth is seen as a weapon and discourse as an assembly of polemical and strategic facts.*' (Foucault, 2014)

Foucault found that, increasingly, modern forms of power require people to govern themselves through practices of the self. The question of how people speak the truth about themselves preoccupied a series of lectures that Foucault delivered at the Catholic University of Louvain, Belgium, in 1981, three years before his death. In these lectures, he examined one practice of veridiction: *avowal*. This is a practice whereby persons affirm a truth that they themselves believe, often in a legal setting. His interest in avowal stemmed from the way that subjects who *avow* are actually producing a specific action. This action is performed by a subject in a very concrete manner that has legal ramifications.

For Foucault, the action of avowal has certain conditions which tie that person, through the act of avowing, to a set of obligations and relations. These obligations make persons into a particular form of subject. A person who avows is undertaking the act of affirming a truth. The action places the speaking subject in a relationship to others who listen to that truth, such as a jury or a judge. It is for this audience that a truth is avowed. The subject has a truth that is affirmed. The act of affirmation makes a subject responsible for that truth.

As such, subjects govern themselves by speaking and knowing this truth. They *create a truth about their self* that is knowable and affirmable. For Foucault, it is through this practice that persons come to constitute themselves as subjects in relation to both ethics and the law. These persons are, through the act of avowal, subsequently treated as responsible for their conduct and the truth that they avow. It is only through these practices that persons can be seen as ethical or legal subjects.

The Christian Confession

Foucault saw that the Christian practice of confession binds a subject to his or her own truth. To confess is to speak the truth about one's own existence, experience and actions. Through confession, people put their experience into discourse in the company of a listener who offers spiritual guidance. Foucault said that the practice of confession should be seen as a 'ritual of discourse'. As a ritual, it has rules, a prescribed order, and specific cultural purposes. But why did Foucault think that confessing was an interesting practice? And how does the practice illustrate a history of truth-telling activities?

Foucault argued that the practice of confession has been the preeminent technique in Western societies for producing truth and knowledge about sexuality. The practice of confession developed among Christian monastic communities during the medieval ages. It was one among other practices, each of which led members of those communities towards self-examination, guidance and obedience (Elden, 2016).

Foucault linked his interest in the practice of confession with a more general concern with the history of the subject and the self. He gave further context for his interest in confessional practice during a lecture delivered at Dartmouth College, USA, in November 1980, titled 'Christianity and Confession'. In this lecture, he sets out the Christian underpinnings of confession: 'As everybody knows, Christianity is a confession' (Foucault, 2007), and, in Christianity, there is an 'obligation to truth'.

Foucault found that the practice of confession was also closely related to the principle of obedience to a teacher. As several Foucault scholars have argued:

'Unlike heathen philosophy, where the relation between teacher and pupil was limited and instrumental because the pupils' temporary obedience was based on the teacher guiding them to a happy and autonomous mode of life, the requirement for obedience in monastic institutions applied to all aspects of life and lasted until death.'
(Raffnsøe, Thaning, and Gudmand-Hoyer, 2016)

Foucault found that monastic communities would relate the practice of confession to the Christian principle that people should be concerned with a 'renunciation of this world and of oneself' (Elden, 2016). By confessing to a truth, people relinquished the hold that their actions have upon them, they would submit those actions to higher ethical values, and thus unburden themselves of those actions taken in 'this' world.

The practice of confession also involves a set of power relations between the confessor and those to whom he or she confesses. A confession is not made in isolation. If you confess to a truth without having anyone listen to your speech, the ritual of confession is not complete. What is interesting about this practice for Foucault is that a hidden truth is confessed to someone else. A listener's relation to the confession establishes a set of power relations. These relations enable the listener to interpret and guide the confession. This means that the interpreter of the confession has a 'hermeneutic function' (Foucault, 1990a). The listener is accomplished in an art of interpretation, knows how to read signs, pick up on clues, listen closely, derive meaning from the confession and, as a result, offer guidance.

What is the order of this ritual? Firstly, the listener asks for a confession. Then, while listening to and interpreting the secrets revealed in the confession, the listener 'prescribes and appreciates it, and intervenes in order to judge, punish, forgive, console and reconcile' (Foucault, 1998). Lastly, the confession is mediated through the interpretations of the listener, which produces a truth about the speaker's self.

The practice of confession is also an important precursor for the Victorian sciences of sexuality. As Foucault outlined in the first volume of *The History of Sexuality*, the practice of confession was incorporated into scientific trials and the production of scientific knowledge. The confession was a precursor to research and diagnostic interviews, psychoanalytic sessions, and other techniques for gathering accounts about sexual practices. The practice of confession was transformed with the introduction of a new type of listener (a qualified practitioner) who would interpret the confessed actions using psychoanalytic concepts. All this was done to interpret the confession and uncover its meaning for the speaker.

From its roots in monastic communities, the practice of confession has subsequently spread much more widely. Foucault went so far as to say that the practice of confession is ubiquitous in the modern world. Confessing is performed in public and in private, to everyone and anyone. As he wrote:

> *'The confession has spread its effects far and wide. It plays a part in justice, medicine, education, family relationships, and love relations, in the most ordinary affairs of everyday life, and in the most solemn rites;*

one confesses one's crimes, one's sins, one's thoughts and desires, one's illnesses and troubles; one goes about telling, with the greatest precision, whatever is most difficult to tell.' (Foucault, 1998)

As we have seen from earlier chapters, the relation between the confessor and the listener allows Foucault to describe the manifestation of truth in a relationship of power, knowledge and discourse. In the practice of confession, the relation is between a confessor and interpreter, a pupil and teacher, a patient and doctor. Foucault saw the practice of confession not as an act of individualistic liberation, but as a ritual for producing a subject's truth through the interpretation of signs.

For Foucault, the modern subject is obliged to know his or her own truth. He said that we need to understand that this truth is produced through specific historical practices. The practice of confession is just one of many other practices where the truth of the self is produced. Other ethical practices – such as avowal, penance, speaking frankly and freely – each involve a different ritual for constituting the subject through an act of producing truth. Some of these practices have been incorporated into other institutions, such as in legal proceedings.

Foucault's philosophy is concerned with how subjects are formed through power and discourse. He considered a modern European philosophical tradition whereby knowing oneself has been given priority over caring for the self. In this tradition, the ethical duty to 'know oneself' is not so much about deconstruction, in the sense of tracing the history of the self's construction. Instead, it is the duty to examine the truth of one's own existence and become an ethical subject. Persons are, effectively, given the duty to govern their selves through self-mastery, knowledge of oneself, and acknowledging one's truths. Foucault writes about this as *persons governing their own souls*, in contrast with being governed by external sources, such as by guards in prisons.

For Foucault, ethical practice is only possible when a truth is produced and known. 'Knowing ourselves' is our primary ethical duty; it is how we govern ourselves. Foucault shows us that when we speak and learn the truth about ourselves, we do not become liberated from a relation of power and knowledge. By speaking our truth we govern our souls.

Conclusion

With Foucault's vision of prisons and asylums, discipline and confessionals, we are offered a unique starting point for philosophy. He asks us to consider how people become who they are and to become aware of the history of the modern subject. His originality does not solely lie in his analysis of power and knowledge, nor in his approach to writing philosophy and history, but in offering a methodology for asking philosophical and political questions of the historical present.

Foucault's questions remain remarkably contemporary. In an era of so-called post-truth politics, scientific skepticism, alternative facts, conspiracy theories, and echo chambers, where there is a growing mistrust of expertise, a resurgence of far-right identity politics, and where citizens are heavily surveilled and policed, Foucault's philosophy provides a guide through those times. Foucault showed how power and knowledge are historically interrelated, how power operates in modern societies, and how practices create new forms of human existence. And although we seem to live in an era where the Enlightenment project of universal reason and scientific progress has 'run aground' against the primacy of feelings (Davies, 2018), Foucault offers his ideas as a map for understanding the foundations of those human sciences that are pervasively influential in public debates and governmental action.

Foucault wrote histories of the present. These are not histories written for the sake of understanding the past, but for interrogating today's truths. This is a philosophy that uncovers past conflicts and contestations to diagnose contemporary life. But, as David Garland writes, 'As always, the historical record yields up its secrets only to those who know precisely how to ask' (Garland, 2014). With his invention of a new mode of philosophy, Foucault's ideas should transform our understanding of both truth and knowledge. As one of Foucault's collaborators, Arlette Farge, wrote, 'The archives do not necessarily tell the truth, but, as Michel Foucault would say, they tell of the truth' (Farge, 2013). These archives evoke and leave traces of the past, they don't speak for themselves.

Foucault also showed us that our present may well have been different. To understand why it is as it is, we need to do historical work. We need to look in our archives. This work, Foucault wrote, 'is grey, meticulous, and patiently documentary' (1977). This is the work of piecing together the remnants of multiple histories found in our culture's archives, libraries, and documents. Whether those histories are found in prison or school records, diaries, government files, journals, caches of letters, the historian who examines these archives finds histories that have been hidden, excluded and forgotten.

Even today, Foucault's ideas continue to provoke debate in academic communities. For the disciplines that make up the social sciences, such as anthropology, sociology, psychology and criminology, his contributions have stimulated debates about the ubiquity of power in all social relations. Foucault showed how the relation between power and knowledge has an instrumental role in constructing social and political realities. Whether we are asking about how power operates in modern societies or how we tell the truth about ourselves, Foucault has left us a novel understanding of both discourse and historical research. He offered more than a method for analyzing historical documents. Following Foucault, we should examine commonly held assumptions about the emergence of truth and knowledge within our society.

Foucault's ideas have also led to new research about crime and punishment. As a result of his work, we also need to acknowledge that power does not simply operate through the imposition of rules and discipline, but through the government of oneself and one's conduct. Scholars such as Alexandra Cox (2018) have written about how young men in the juvenile justice system are required to examine their selves and exercise practices of self-control as an everyday aspect of incarceration. Other scholarship continues to draw from Foucault's *The History of Sexuality*, bringing his ideas together with feminism and intersectional analysis to examine the historical constitution of sex offenders, sexual offences and re-offending (Taylor, 2018).

New scholarship on Foucault's life and ideas continues to appear. Recent intellectual histories by Stuart Elden, titled *Foucault's Last Decade* (2016) and *Foucault: The Birth of Power* (2017), draw from untranslated writings Foucault's archive held in the Bibliothèque Nationale in France, and Foucault's unpublished manuscripts. Newly translated editions of Foucault's writings and lectures, such as the 2018 publication of the fourth volume of *The History of Sexuality*, titled *Confessions of the Flesh* (the original title being *Les Aveux de la Chair*), has stimulated recent debates about his ideas.

By tracing the contours of Foucault's life and thought, readers can look more broadly at other philosophical debates in the 20th century. Readers are encouraged to further explore the figures behind his varied collaborations and debates, such as Gilles Deleuze, Jacques Derrida, Arlette Farge and George Jackson. This book has shown that Foucault wrote on a wide variety of subjects, as diverse as prisoners' rights, sexual liberation, the nature of madness, phenomenology, ethics, aesthetics. For interested readers there are a plethora of starting points to pursue.

This book is part of a series called *Who the hell is…?* and Michel Foucault's contribution to philosophy belongs alongside the other Classical and Modern philosophers who form part of this series, such as Aristotle, Plato, Nietzsche and Hume. Foucault is a philosopher of the 20th century, whose questions were not scholastic, arid or purely cerebral. When Foucault cast himself as a diagnostician, he did not claim that he had discovered a cure or a treatment. What he offered was a history of our present, a meticulous philosophical examination of how we arrived at this particular historical juncture. So, after his diagnoses, Foucault offered neither magic potions nor surgical instruments, but an open invitation to the archives and new genealogies.

Bibliography

Works by Foucault

Foucault, M. (1963) *Death and the Labyrinth: The World of Raymond Roussel*. London: Athlone Press.

Foucault, M. (1976) *The History of Sexuality* (trans. Robert Hurley). New York: Pantheon Books.

Foucault, M. (1984–1985). 'Dream, imagination and existence'. *Review of Existential Psychology & Psychiatry*, 19(1), 29–78.

Foucault, M. (1977) 'Nietzsche, Genealogy, History' in *Language, Counter-Memory, Practice: Selected Essays and Interviews* (ed. D. F. Bouchard). Ithaca: Cornell University Press.

Foucault. M. (1980a) *Power/Knowledge: Selected Interviews and Other Writings 1972–1977* (ed. Colin Gordon). New York: Vintage.

Foucault, M. (1980b) *Herculine Barbin: Being the recently discovered memories of a nineteenth century French hermaphrodite*. New York: Pantheon.

Foucault, M. (1988a) *The Care of the Self. The History of Sexuality, Volume 3* (trans. Robert Hurley). New York: Vintage.

Foucault, M. (1988b) *Technologies of the Self: A Seminar with Michel Foucault* (eds. Luther H. Martin, Huck Gutman and Patrick H. Hutton). Amherst: University of Massachusetts Press.

Foucault, M. (1990a) *The History of Sexuality: An Introduction, Volume 1* (trans. Robert Hurley). New York: Vintage.

Foucault. M. (1990b) *The Use of Pleasure. The History of Sexuality, Volume 2* (trans. Robert Hurley). New York: Random House.

Foucault, M. (1991a) 'Between "words" and "things" during May '68' in *Remarks on Marx: Conversations with Duccio Trombadori*. New York: Semiotext(e).

Foucault, M. (1991b) 'Introduction' in G. Canguilhem, *The Normal and the Pathological* (trans. Caroline R. Fawcett). New York: Zone Books.

Foucault. M. (1991c) *Discipline and Punish: The Birth of the Prison* (trans. Ian Sheridan). London: Penguin.

Foucault, M. (1992) *The Archaeology of Knowledge and the Discourse on Language*. New York: Vintage.

Foucault, M. (1994a) *Dits et Ecrits* (4 volumes). Paris: Gallimard.

Foucault, M. (1994b) *Ethics: Subjectivity and Truth: Essential Works of Michel Foucault 1954-1984 Volume 1* (eds. Paul Rabinow, James D Faubion). Paris: Gallimard.

Foucault, M. (1997) 'On the Genealogy of Ethics: An Overview of Work in Progress' in *Ethics, Subjectivity and Truth* (ed. P. Rabinow). London: Penguin.

Foucault, M. (2001) *The Order of Things: Archaeology of the Human Sciences*. Abingdon: Routledge.

Foucault, M. (2003) *'Society Must Be Defended': Lectures at the Collège de France 1975–1976* (trans. David Macey). New York: Picador.

Foucault, M. (2006a) *The Hermeneutics of the Subject: Lectures at the Collège de France 1981–1982* (trans. Graham Burchell). New York: Picador.

Foucault, M. (2006b) *Psychiatric Power: Lectures at the Collège de France 1973–1974* (trans. Graham Burchell). New York: Palgrave Macmillan.

Foucault, M. (2007) *The Politics of Truth* (ed. Sylvere Lotringer, trans. Lisa Hochroth & Catherine Porter). Los Angeles, CA: Semiotext(e).

Foucault, M. (2012a) *The Birth of the Clinic: An Archaeology of Medical Perception* (trans. Alan Sheridan Smith). New York: Vintage Books.

Foucault, M. (2012b) 'Michel Foucault: Freedom and Knowledge' in *Freedom and Knowledge: a Hitherto Unpublished Interview* (ed. F. Elders, trans. Lionel Claris). Amsterdam: NUR.

Foucault, M. (2013a) *Speech Begins After Death* (trans. Roberto Bonnono). Minneapolis: University of Minnesota Press.

Foucault, M. (2013b) *Lectures on the Will to Know: Lectures at the College de France 1970-1971 with Oedipal Knowledge.* Basingstoke: Palgrave-Macmillan.

Foucault, M. (2013c) 'Preface' to G. Deleuze and F. Guattari, F. *Anti-Oedipus: Capitalism and Schizophrenia.* London: Bloomsbury.

Foucault, M. (2014) *Wrong-Doing, Truth-Telling: The Function of Avowal in Justice* (eds. Fabienne Brion and Bernard E. Harcourt). Chicago: University of Chicago Press.

Foucault, M. (2015) *The Punitive Society: Lectures at the Collège de France, 1972–1973.* New York: Palgrave Macmillan.

Foucault, M. (2016a) *Abnormal: Lectures at the Collège de France 1974–1975* (trans. Graham Burchell). London: Verso.

Foucault, M., Artieres, P., et al. (2016b) *Speech Begins After Death.* Minnesota: University of Minnesota Press.

Foucault, M. (2019) 'Lives of Infamous Men' [1977] in *Archives of Infamy: Foucault on State Power in the Lives of Ordinary Citizens* (ed. N. Luxon). Minneapolis: University of Minnesota Press.

Other works cited

Blanchot, M. (1987) 'Michel Foucault as I Imagine Him' in *Foucault/Blanchot: Maurice Blanchot: The Thought from Outside and Michel Foucault As I Imagine Him* (trans. Jeffrey Mehlman and Brian Massumi). New York: Zone Books.

Bonnefoy, C. (2002). *Le Beau Danger, Entretien avec Claude Bonnefoy.* Paris: éditions de l'EHESS.

Brunon-Ernst, M.A. (2012) 'Introduction' to *Beyond Foucault: New Perspectives on Bentham's Panopticon* (ed. M.A. Brunon-Ernst). Farnham: Ashgate Publishing Ltd.

Caluya, G. (2010) 'The post-panoptic society? Reassessing Foucault in surveillance studies.' *Social Identities* 16(5).

Canguilhem, G. (1966) *The Normal and the Pathological.* Paris: Presses Universitaires de France.

Chang, J.H. (2014) 'Multiple Power in Colonial Spaces.' *ABE Journal. Architecture beyond Europe*, (5).

Cox, A. (2018) *Trapped in a Vice: The Consequences of Confinement for Young People.* Brunswick: Rutgers University Press.

Davies, W. (2018) *Nervous States: How Feeling Took Over the World.* London: Random House.

Defert, D. (2013) 'Chronology' in *A Companion to Foucault* (eds. C. Falzon, T. O'Leary & J. Sawicki). Chichester: Wiley-Blackwell.

Deleuze, G. (1988) *Foucault.* London: Continuum.

Deleuze, G. (1992) 'Postscript on the Societies of Control'. *October*, Vol. 59.

Deleuze, G. (2004) *Desert Islands: And Other Texts, 1953–1974.* Los Angeles: Semiotext(e).

Derrida, J. (2003) *The Work of Mourning.* Chicago: University of Chicago Press.

Elden, S. (2016) *Foucault's Last Decade.* London: Polity.

Elden, S., (2017) *Foucault: The Birth of Power.* London: Polity.

Elden, S. (2018) 'Michel Foucault, Histoire de la sexualité 4: Les aveux de la chair'. *Theory, Culture & Society*, 35 (7–8).

Eribon, D. (1992) *Michel Foucault.* (trans. by Betsy Wing). Cambridge: Harvard University Press.

Farge, A. (2013) *The Allure of the Archives.* New Haven: Yale University Press.

Garland, D. (1985) *Punishment and Welfare: A History of Penal Strategies.* Aldershot: Ashgate.

Garland, D. (2014) 'What is a "history of the present"? On Foucault's genealogies and their critical preconditions.' *Punishment & Society,* 16(4).

Gilliam, C. (2018) 'Vrais Amis: Reconsidering the Philosophical Relationship Between Foucault and Deleuze'. *Foucault Studies,* 25(2).

Gordon, C. (2016) 'Foucault: The Materiality of a Working Life. An interview with Daniel Defert' by Alain Brossat, assisted by Philippe Chevallier. *Foucault Studies,* 21.

Graham, S. (2011) *Cities Under Siege: The New Military Urbanism.* London: Verso Books.

Guibert, H. (1995) *To The Friend Who Did Not Save My Life.* London: Quartet Books.

Heiner, B.T.(2007) 'Foucault and the Black Panthers'. *City,* 11(3).

Kafka, F. (1988) *The Diaries of Franz Kafka.* New York: Schocken Books.

Legg, S. (2007) 'Beyond the European province: Foucault and Postcolonialism' in *Space, Knowledge and Power: Foucault and Geography* (eds. J.W. Crampton and S. Elden). Aldershot: Ashgate.

Luxon, N. (2019) *Archives of Infamy: Foucault on State Power in the Lives of Ordinary Citizens.* Minneapolis: University of Minnesota Press.

Macey, D. (2019) *The Lives of Michel Foucault.* London: Verso.

Medien, K. (2019) 'Foucault in Tunisia: The encounter with intolerable power'. *The Sociological Review,* 27 August 2019.

Michael, D. (1982) 'Foucault's Genealogy of the Human Sciences'. *Economy and Society,* 11(4).

Miller, J. (2000) *The Passion of Michel Foucault.* Cambridge: Harvard University Press.

Miller, J. (1990) 'Foucault: The Secrets of a Man'. *Salmagundi,* 88-89, Fall 1990–Winter 1991.

Mitchell, T. (1991) *Colonising Egypt.* Berkeley: University of California Press.

Rabinow, P. (2011) *The Accompaniment: Assembling the Contemporary.* Chicago: University of Chicago Press.Raffnsøe, S., Thaning, M.S. and Gudmand-Hoyer, M. (2016) *Michel Foucault: A Research Companion.* Basingstoke: Palgrave Macmillan.

Redfield, P. (2005) 'Foucault in the Tropics: Displacing the Panopticon' in *Anthropologies of Modernity: Foucault, Governmentality, and Life Politics* (ed. J.X. Inda). Malden: Blackwell.

Ricardo, D. (1817) *On The Principles of Political Economy and Taxation.* London: John Murray.

Taylor, C. (2018) *Foucault, Feminism, and Sex Offences: An Anti-Carceral Analysis.* New York: Routledge.

Pettit, P. (1975) *The Concept of Structuralism: A Critical Analysis.* Berkeley: University of California Press.

Wood, D.M. (2007) 'Beyond the Panopticon? Foucault and surveillance studies' in *Space, Knowledge and Power: Foucault and Geography* (eds. J.W. Crampton and S. Elden). London: Routledge.

Biography

Julian Molina is the author of research articles on social problems work, administrative proceedings, the uses of social scientific evidence, and ethnomethodology. He holds a PhD in Sociology from the University of Warwich, and is a graduate of Goldsmiths, University of London. Julian lives in London, England.

Acknowledgements

This book was developed after a welcome push from Penny Huntsman. I thank the publishers of Bowden & Brazil Ltd, Alice Bowden and Sarah Tomley, for their support, feedback and patience. Thanks to Jonathan Birch for his comments on the full manuscript. Along the way I received significant help from Thomas Percival and Elaine Wedlock. And, to unnamed others, 'Remember, she who keepeth the Books runneth the Business'.

Who the hell is

This exciting new series of books sets out to explore the life and theories of the world's leading intellectuals in a clear and understandable way. The series currently includes the following subject areas:

Art History | Psychology | Philosophy | Sociology | Politics

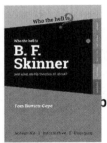

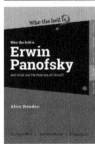

For more information about forthcoming titles in the Who the hell is...? series, go to: **www.whothehellis.co.uk**.

If any of our readers would like to put in a request for a particular intellectual to be included in our series, then please contact us at **info@whothehellis.co.uk**.

Printed in Great Britain
by Amazon

57742435R00073